GLENN PATMORE teaches Constitutional Law and Law of Democracy at the University of Melbourne. He has given invited lectures at international universities such as the London School of Economics and L'Universite Paris-Sorbonne, and has published in a range of Australian and international journals on the topic of republican reform. Glenn participates in republican debates and conferences. He also appeared before the Australian Senate inquiry into an Australian republic in 2004. Many of Glenn's published writings appeal to both an academic and more popular audience.

CHOOSING THE REPUBLIC

GLENN PATMORE

A UNSW Press book

Published by
University of New South Wales Press Ltd
University of New South Wales
Sydney NSW 2052
AUSTRALIA
www.unswpress.com.au

© Glenn Patmore 2009
First published 2009

This book is copyright. Apart from any fair dealing for the purpose of private study, research, criticism or review, as permitted under the Copyright Act, no part may be reproduced by any process without written permission. Inquiries should be addressed to the publisher.

National Library of Australia
Cataloguing-in-Publication entry
Author: Patmore, G. A. (Glenn Anthony), 1961-
Title: Choosing the republic / Glenn Patmore.
ISBN: 9781742230153 (pbk.)
Notes: Includes index.
Subjects: Republicanism – Australia.
　　　　　Democracy – Australia.
　　　　　Representative government and representation – Australia.
　　　　　Australia – Politics and government.
Dewey Number:　320.494

Design Di Quick
Printer Ligare

This book is printed on paper using fibre supplied from plantation or sustainably managed forests.

Contents

Acknowledgments *vii*
Introduction *1*
1 The 200-year drought *9*
2 Raising the question *21*
3 Altering the Australian Constitution *31*
4 Glimpsing the Governor-General *63*
5 The politics of minimalism *89*
6 Between participation and neutrality: selecting the head of state *112*
7 (Mis)behaviour in republican Australia *145*
8 Ask the leaders and the people *174*
9 The incurable republic *198*
Notes *206*
Index *233*

Acknowledgments

This book has benefited enormously from interviews with leaders in the republican debate, including: former Prime Minister Paul Keating; former Leader of the Opposition Kim Beazley; former Liberal Member of Parliament Bob Charles; delegates to the 1998 Constitutional Convention, Jason Yat-sen Li, Phil Cleary, Sir David Smith and Professor Greg Craven; former Prime Minister John Howard; and former Executive Director of Australians for Constitutional Monarchy Kerry Jones. Each of the interviewees was incredibly generous with their time and I thank them sincerely.

Special thanks must be given to Associate Professor Jeremy Gans and Ms Mas Generis who guided me through the University of Melbourne's ethics process for conducting interviews.

A very special debt is owed to Professor John D Whyte, the co-author of my first article on Australian republicanism. His work has had a profound influence on the writing in this volume, particularly his conception of the constitutional guarantor.

In the preparation of this manuscript I was adeptly aided by part-time research assistants who read material to me, found sources, transcribed interviews and offered thoughtful comments. I am extremely grateful to Derek Finch, Holly Smart, Luke Forster, Natasha McNamara, Shu Qing Tan, Alexandra Whelan, Tom Andrews, Chula na Ranong and Genevieve Grant. Special thanks to Sarah Shrub and Jody Lee who read earlier drafts and offered thoughtful comments.

After I submitted the first draft to my publisher, I was ably assisted by the new Law Library Research Service. A very special thanks to Alissa Sputore, Law Research Service Manager, and her fine research assistant Elly Patira. I am also indebted to my copyeditor Alison Savage for her thoughtful suggestions and comments.

I am grateful to the Melbourne Law School, which provided me with research funding. In particular, I would like to thank Deputy Dean Simon Evans and Sub Dean Research Carolyn Evans for their support of this project. Publication of this work was also assisted by a publication grant from the University of Melbourne.

Some parts of this book draw upon previous publications. However, these essays have been modified and developed in the writing of this book. The original publications are:

> G Patmore (2006) 'Choosing the Republic: The Legal and Constitutional Steps in Australia and Canada', *Queen's Law Journal*, vol. 31, pp. 270–95.
>
> G Patmore (2003) 'The Head of State as Guarantor of Democratic Government' in *The Big Makeover: A New Australian Constitution: Labor Essays*, (ed.) G Patmore, Pluto Press Australia, pp. 174–95.
>
> G Patmore and J Whyte (1997) 'Imagining Constitutional Crises: Power and (Mis)behaviour in Republican Australia', *Federal Law Review*, vol. 25, pp. 181–203.

Finally, I am especially grateful to the University of New South Wales Press for their support and enthusiasm in publishing this book. I would like to specially mention Phillipa McGuinness, Chantal Gibbs and Heather Cam.

Introduction

If ever there was a moment in history that called for a republic, it was the late 1990s. We were on the cusp of a new millennium. Sydney was about to host the 2000 Olympics and Australia was preparing to celebrate 100 years of Federation. Despite the climate for change, the 1999 republican referendum still failed. Similarly today, a commonly held view is that Australia will not become a republic until the Queen abdicates, or there is a new monarch in England. Yet surely these great historical events are the happenstance of history. Creating a republic might certainly coincide with such moments but its timing ought not to depend on the hand of chance.

To be a republican is to believe that we must instigate and plan the reform ourselves. In the 1990s some saw themselves as the proponents of change, and gave voice to the republic.[1] Many showed their support by voting in the 1999 referendum and many would like to vote again. There were, of course, advocates of the status quo. There were also those seeking more significant constitutional change. And those who offered resistance to the republican proposal ultimately triumphed.[2]

Although the 1999 referendum was unsuccessful, it engaged the people in a debate that spanned a decade. The debate involved serious consideration of a proposal, our imaginations of ourselves and the political future of our nation. Given that November 2009 is the tenth anniversary of the republican referendum, it is timely to revisit the issue.

I believe that through becoming a republic we can create a more democratic and independent future for ourselves. This book is motivated by that belief. Only by examining our past can we chart a new direction for our future, and if we wish to understand the future of republicanism we need to know something of the views of the leaders and the people from then and now. This book is infused with their voices, doubts, aspirations, and proposed alternatives.

This is not a book about assigning personal responsibility for the failure of the referendum. Rather, the book draws on the views of the leaders to find lessons for the future. And the critical lesson is that the democratic process has and will continue to influence the republican reform debate. Given that the choice of the people is the hallmark of Western democracies like Australia, the question considered in this book is how the people in a constitutional monarchy may choose to become a republic. But before the people can choose a republican head of state we must have a reinvigorated public debate. Accordingly, this book is both a call for renewed political, legal and policy debates, and offers a straightforward guide to republican reform for the general public.

Themes

The first theme explores the history of political republicanism in Australia. Historically, republicanism has always formed part of Australia's social fabric, even if it has been steadfastly avoided for over 200 years by most political leaders. We can learn much from the views of the leaders in the 1990s, their proposals for republican reform and their impact on public opinion.

This book then goes on to examine the process of altering the Constitution. Proposals for change are put into the public consciousness by our leaders, and critical steps here include an initiation of proposals, selection of a model, informing the people and the formal process of constitutional amendment. Popular choice requires that the people must be engaged by each of these steps.

The third theme focuses on constitutional design. It is important to understand the functions of the

Governor-General in order to appreciate the alternative proposals for a non-executive President. This book will examine the Keating and 1999 referendum bipartisan parliamentary election models, and consider proposals for direct election. In order to develop effective and convincing proposals for the future, it is not simply a matter of altering the text of the Constitution. Important questions must be asked, such as: How should republican philosophy influence proposals for change? What is the role of a citizen in a republic? How should the office of head of state embody principles of participation and stability? The book addresses these issues from the perspective of popular participation in the choices that are open to us.

The final theme explored is that of the debate itself. Various republican proposals are looked at in detail, to distinguish the important issues involved with a parliamentary and a popularly elected head of state. But it is up to the reader to form their own opinion about their preferred model. It is also important to consider the views and opinions of republican and monarchist leaders, as well as the general public, in order to understand just why the 1999 referendum failed. Nationalism, voter comprehension and education, trust and popular participation are all important aspects to explore.

After more than 100 years of Federation, Australia has developed a unique parliamentary democracy that many Australians are proud of and wish to retain. There is also evidence that, overwhelmingly, Australians want to retain our democratic system.³ We should not be surprised by this. In a 2008 Australian National University poll, 81 per cent of respondents were very or fairly satisfied with how democracy works in Australia.⁴ Even so, others have argued for the adoption of an American or French model, primarily because it would involve a stricter separation between the government and the Parliament. My view is that we should continue with our current non-executive head of state with its responsive parliamentary system of government. Under that system, the Prime Minister and Cabinet are answerable to the Parliament and ultimately the people. The challenge for republicans is to establish a new head of state which is significant enough without attempting to introduce elements from other systems that might unsettle Australia's distinct form of democracy.

Definitions

One of our tasks in reinvigorating the republican debate is to understand the significance of key terms such as democracy, popular choice and republicanism. These words have a strong rhetorical flavour yet each can be distilled.

Representative democracy is where the people rule by either directly or indirectly choosing their representatives. Through this process of representative democracy, official constitutional and political change is initiated, opportunities for participation and discussion are created, the questions of constitutional reform are formulated and, ultimately, the people are given their say.

Direct democracy is also vital, for it is through this process that voters may have a say in plebiscites and referendums. In plebiscites, the electors are asked to vote on a question of national importance, whereas in a referendum to amend the Australian Constitution,[5] electors are asked to vote on a law that is referred to them for their final approval.[6] There is a vital intersection between representative and direct democracy. The Parliament proposes and the electors decide.

The Constitution provides for popular choice in the procedure for electing representatives and appointing Ministers. The people directly choose their members of Parliament,[7] although the choice of the Prime Minister and Ministers is indirect, namely through parliamentary representatives.[8] Control over policy by the electors is also through representatives.[9]

Popular choice also means the expressed preference of the people as electors,[10] citizens,[11] or 'members of the constitutional community'.[12] As elected officials, Ministers make decisions on behalf of the people and, in this sense, Ministers make popular choices, for they are of the people and are given the authority to speak for us. Ministers are also responsive to the views of electors, since 'popular influence over policy' occurs day in day out.[13] This influence may take different forms, such as through the popular media, community groups, elites and even State parliamentarians. We should not underestimate the influence of leaders of community groups, such as the Australian Republican Movement and Australians for Constitutional Monarchy. As Professor John McMillan has pointed out, politicians and leaders possess a 'public legitimacy', and 'are practised in the art of distilling the mood and persuading the mind of a diverse and fractious electorate'. These leaders have 'a decisive role to play in constitutional change'.[14] Therefore, policy-makers, representatives and Ministers who initiate political and constitutional change must respond to the popular will.

Popular choice operates differently under conditions of direct and indirect democracy. When voting in referendums to change the Constitution, electors make policy choices; they exert control over the decision to alter the Constitution. Even though the question is ultimately framed by the Federal Parliament, a referendum ought not be regarded merely as a choice offered to the people, but one in which they ought to be engaged throughout the entire process of change. Indeed, lack of appreciation of the power given to the people under the Constitution resulted in the failure of the 1999 referendum.

Much of this book is concerned with the choices our leaders make because of their constitutional and political roles. But it is also concerned with how the leaders are required to engage with the people under the Constitution. The legal structure and political forces both shape how a choice is put to the people and, more importantly, influence the question asked. Ultimately, the choice of the people will be the critical consideration in achieving republican reform.

But what is republicanism? Republicanism, our last key term, may be defined as:

- a government whose head of state is not a monarch
- a state in which the supreme power lies in citizens who elect their representatives
- respublica, meaning 'public things or affairs' or a body politic committed to the public and common good of all citizens.[15]

'Respublica' is a fluid term that may refer simply to a nation state, either a constitutional monarchy or republic. But in the Australian context, republic is contrasted to monarchy. This opposition is very much part of Australian history, as will be shown in the subsequent political history of republicanism.

Choosing the Republic then is an historical, constitutional and legal study of political republicanism in Australia. It is also an examination of referendum democracy in practice; its goals and features. And finally, the book reflects upon the critical choices of the leaders and the people, and considers their implications for the future.

1

The 200-year drought

The Commonwealth is the official title of the Australian Government, but it's a little known fact that it's also part of the title of the Australian Constitution. It's even less well known that the term is steeped in republican history.

At the time of Federation in 1901, the word 'Commonwealth' was associated with a revolutionary period of English history when England was ruled without a monarch. This period was known as Cromwell's Protectorate. On 19 March 1649, well before the American Declaration of Independence, Oliver Cromwell's Parliament established a republic and proclaimed England to be a:

> Commonwealth or Free State … by the supreme authority of this nation, the representatives of the

> people in parliament, and by such as they shall constitute officers and ministers under them for the good of the people and without any king or House of Lords.[1]

Whether this was a common person's uprising or a *coup d'état*, the protectorate must have sent a shockwave through the monarchies of Europe. Indeed, according to folklore, Queen Victoria had to be consoled at the thought that Australia might become a Commonwealth when the *Constitution Act 1900* was sent to the United Kingdom for royal assent!

Colonial politicians and writers at the time were quick to downplay the republican and revolutionary connotations.[2] Two men closely associated with the movement for Federation, Sir John Quick and Sir Robert Garran, writing after 1901, felt the term only 'jarred upon some ears with a slight revolutionary echo … but its older and deeper meaning soon prevailed, and it stands today for the type and the ideal of Australian nationhood'.[3]

What, then, was that older and deeper meaning? According to Quick and Garran it was the common 'derivation of the term "common" and "weal", or "wealth"; it signified common wellbeing or common good'.[4] The prospect of a common wealth is what embodied the spirit of Federation. It was a political slogan writ large that moved colonists to vote for Federation, a perfect sound bite for the times. Quick and Garran, in the romantic language of the Victorians, describe the poignant effect of the term:

> It is not too much to say that this grand old word, rich in meaning and tradition, and intimately associated with the literature and history of the English people, did more to arrest the public attention and kindle the public imagination than any other word in the English language could have done.[5]

The older meaning of the common good is steeped in republican philosophy too, yet its deeper republican or overtly egalitarian meaning has been gradually lost. The term 'commonwealth' is now more a title than an aspiration. Constitutional writers also use it to describe a set of political relationships in a very technical way. At Federation, it was a term used to describe the Commonwealth as a self-governing colony, not yet a fully fledged nation state.[6] It was also a term used to describe the central government as opposed to the governments of the States.[7]

Republicanism has faded from the view of constitutional history, as the term 'commonwealth' illustrates. Yet, its spirit may inhabit the Australian Federation more than in some other countries. The political history of Australian republicanism raises a vital question for us today. Why did so many Australian political leaders steadfastly avoid republicanism for over 200 years? With the benefit of hindsight, this prolonged avoidance seems quite extraordinary. Was it simply a sentimental attachment to the British Empire? Or did the allegiance to the monarchy rest on deeper political and economic ties? Perhaps republicanism was just too revolutionary for the new Australian British leaders of their times!

Avoiding the 'R' word

For over 200 years Australian political leaders have supported constitutional monarchy and, for many, there has been no desire to advocate for constitutional change to introduce a republic.[8] In fact, it could be argued that there has been a steadfast shunning of the 'R' word.[9] In early colonial Australia, there were three dangerous 'R' words: republicanism, rebellion and revolution. For the King's Governors in the Australian colonies, republicanism was an anathema, a term not mentioned in 'civilised society' since it carried the connotation of rebellion, 'an attack on the person and symbol of the Crown'.[10] After the bloody American and French revolutions, republicanism became associated with the overthrow of a government. And as revolutionary sentiment did exist in Australia, to be a colonial republican was tantamount to treason.[11]

In those days, republicans were perceived as being dangerous and, much like today's terrorists, were liable to prosecution for the crime of sedition: speaking or writing with an intention to bring into hatred, contempt or incite dissatisfaction against the Sovereign (including the King or government). In 1806, for instance, one republican was convicted of sedition and sentenced to a brutal punishment: 100 lashes and banishment to the coal mines at Newcastle. That punishment was not sufficient, however, and 'the prisoner had to be shamed':[12] on the way to the mines he was made to wear a label on which 'Thomas Paine' was written in large letters.[13] Tom Paine, an English-born advocate for American revolution, was renowned in the Australian colony[14] for his 'seditious' book, *The Rights of Man*.[15] The mere mention of these 'indefeasible rights' at a protest meeting, which invoked the spirit of French republicanism, unleashed an impassioned criticism by the editor of the *Australian*:[16] 'The terrible example of the French Revolution ... that nation which got drunk with blood to vomit crime should teach all men the danger of these monstrous doctrines.'[17]

Yet the opportunity to promote sedition and advocate revolutionary republicanism was limited by the presence of British marines. Until at least the 1840s, colonial New South Wales was a garrison society protected by muskets and sabres.[18]

In the middle part of the nineteenth century, republicanism in the colonies became associated with another rebellious movement, the Irish struggle for independence.[19] While there was some support in Australia for Irish independence, that support was opposed by a surge in loyalist sentiment in the late 1860s.[20] By this time, too, colonial leaders had become captivated by a new vision of colonial independence: the self-governing colony.[21] Representation with the power to tax was enshrined in the colonial constitutions. Yet, the Australian colonies' self-governance remained subject to the overriding laws of the Imperial Parliament, the so-called 'laws of paramount force'. These were special laws that prevailed over colonial laws. For Australian republicans, the choice between dependence and independence was no longer as 'politically or rhetorically clear'.[22] The self-governing colony was, in fact, a conservative compromise: it preserved the rule of the British Empire but also gave a measure of real independence.

The revolutionary face of republicanism had softened too. Republicans were no longer just seen as dangerous; they were regarded more as iconoclasts, 'a bravurist political sect opposed to the dominant political culture of sober constitutional monarchy'.[23] In 1887, for instance, republicans in Sydney disrupted meetings set up to plan celebrations for Queen Victoria's jubilee.[24] Some were regarded as convict larrikins, reacting against authority, and some were bordering on the criminal. At one meeting, on 10 June 1887, '[p]olice and loyalists fought open battles with republicans, overturning chairs and tables and removing them forcibly from the meeting. Cries of loyalty to the Queen were met by cheers for separation and an Australian republic'.[25]

In the 1880s there was yet another 'peak' in republicanism, this time focusing on struggles between labour and management and opposed to social inequality.[26] In cities and significant country towns 'fifteen republican organisations and twenty newspapers or journals appeared'.[27] Yet this egalitarian republicanism ultimately failed because it lacked a social program and gave rise to ethnic divisions. Labour leaders as well as loyalists in the government shied away from this divisive republicanism,[28] thereby limiting the options for republicans.

Yet another explanation for the avoidance of the 'R' word by colonial leaders was a new vision for politics in the colonies, one that celebrated the colonies' virtues, but still stressed their ties with Britain. Suffrage for men and women was being strived for,[29] and indeed was granted at a far earlier date in the Australian colonies than in the United Kingdom. In this period, before the depression of the 1890s, Australia was being described as the workingman's paradise, with high wages and the eight-hour day. Its prosperity was built on the gold rush, exploitation of the land and industrialisation. The trade in iron and natural resources strengthened the economic ties between the colony and England, and the Royal Navy largely provided the colonies' defence.[30] The colonies' prosperity and defence were intimately tied up with the economy of the Empire itself. Sir Henry Parkes, the Premier of New South Wales at the time, noted that there was a 'crimson thread of kinship', a sentiment apparently genuinely felt by Britons in Australia.[31]

The meaning of republicanism had undergone a further change too. No longer perceived purely as a rebellious or ratbag movement, it was now a synonym for a fully independent nation state. Some Australian political leaders began to openly speak of Australia in this way. At conventions held to debate the draft Australian Constitution in the 1890s, one delegate, George Dibbs, claimed to have a 'slight tinge' of republicanism.[32] And again at the 1891 National Australasian Convention in Sydney, Dibbs said that 'when [England] planted her colonies in this country she planted them with that germ and spirit of independence which must, as time rolls on, develop into the establishment of a great republic'.[33]

Despite some republican sentiment appearing during these Federation debates, the vast majority of delegates were in no doubt that their constitution should be framed under the British Crown.[34] Accordingly, the high points of constitutional monarchy as a foil to revolutionary republicanism in Australia may be seen as the achievement of self-government and then Federation.[35]

For delegates to the constitutional conventions, Australian nationalism was consistent with loyalty to the Queen.[36] For colonial politicians, such as Alfred Deakin, who became Australia's second Prime Minister, there was no conflict between being Australian and being British. Deakin believed passionately in a dual allegiance to 'colonial nationalism' within an 'imperial unity'.[37]

The strength of monarchist sentiment at Federation was displayed by response to a telegram from Queen Victoria sent to the 1893 Convention: 'Have received your telegram with great satisfaction, and am much pleased at the loyalty evinced on this important occasion. Victoria, Queen and Empress … *Hon. Members gave three cheers for her Majesty the Queen.*'[38]

Post Federation, the Australian Labor Party was loyal to the Crown and the Empire too.[39] Loyalty meant more than three cheers for the Queen, though; it meant that Australians fought and died in the wars of the Empire. Allegiance came with the cost of a huge loss of life in World War I and World War II.[40] Yet it seems that Australian political leaders supported the Empire because of its commitment to 'parliamentary government',[41] as well as from the 'fear of foreign invasion and the associated belief that the British connection offered the best possible protection for Australia's white Pacific enclave'.[42]

By World War II, the military might of the Empire started to crumble, challenged by the rising powers of Germany and Japan. With the capture of fortress Singapore by the Japanese, Royal Britannia no longer ruled the waves. The Australian Government was compelled to pass the *Statute of Westminster Adoption Act 1942* (Cth) to remove legal doubts about the conduct of the Australian war effort due to the existence of Imperial legislation. Australia's international independence grew with the enactment of this statute, enabling Parliament to repeal Imperial laws as well as make laws operating outside Australia. The statute therefore removing two shackles of Empire proving to be a nuisance in the conduct of the war effort.[43]

After World War II, Australia looked to the United States as its new powerful friend and ally. In the early 1950s Liberal Prime Minister Menzies eventually embraced the security agreement with the United States and New Zealand (ANZUS), one which excluded Britain.[44] Yet Menzies' belief in the 'importance ... of Australian loyalty to the throne' remained steadfast, evidenced by his famous recitation in 1963 of an alleged seventeenth-century poet that: 'I did but see her passing by, and yet I love her till I die.'[45]

By the mid-1960s, economic ties with Britain had become less important as markets for Australian goods were developed in Asia.[46] In fact, by the 1970s, it was reported that 'almost half of Australia's markets lay in Asia'.[47] England also became a member of the European Economic Community in 1973, ending the trade preference Commonwealth countries had had with Britain for goods and services.[48]

Separatist republicanism was given a jolt by the constitutional crisis in 1975.[49] Sir John Kerr's dismissal of Labor Prime Minister Gough Whitlam gave rise to fresh demands for constitutional reform and Australian independence. But with the cooling of political passions, the Labor Party's political reforms came to focus more on incremental legal change rather than vigorous calls for an end to the monarchy.

The constitutional and legal ties to Britain were finally severed by the *Australia Act* in 1986. The Act was significant because it made it clear that the United Kingdom no longer exercised legislative, executive or judicial power over Australia. And with little fanfare, or even drama, the High Court of Australia was able to simply declare in 1999 that under our Constitution the United Kingdom was now a 'foreign power'.[50] Of course, one significant constitutional tie remained: the vestigial role of the Queen as head of state.

By the 1990s the old reasons for our political leaders to avoid the 'R' word no longer seemed to make sense. The cultural, legal and economic ties between Australia and Britain were far less important than they once were. The United Kingdom and Australia had grown apart, and Australia was now an independent nation state, a republic in all but name. Today, the monarch's role as head of state in Australian politics has diminished. With the Royal Family taking on the status of celebrities, and the glare of publicity not treating them kindly, the gloss has been further removed.

How times have changed

For over two centuries, Australia's political leaders have tended to keep away from, rather than openly embrace republicanism. The establishment of a republic has been either prevented from happening or avoided by many political leaders, an avoidance that was not based on a political program but an unpalatable idea that has morphed and changed over time.[51] Largely, the resistance has come from a fear of rebellion, disruption, division and disloyalty aroused by the 'R' word. Even when the word became a synonym for a fully independent nation state, the desire to promote this aspiration took well into the twentieth century to achieve. Thus, adoption of the republic is 'a notion of political change which is both propelled and impeded by its own historical baggage'.[52] The republic is driven by nationalist aspirations yet impeded because of the negative connotations of the word. But by the 1990s, some Australian political leaders were ready to discard the old historical baggage!

Where once being a republican was associated with rebellion and revolution, today it is, for many, the mark of a true patriot. This change of attitude became particularly clear in the early 1990s as we witnessed our political leaders openly advocating the birth of a bold political idea: Australia the republic.

2

Raising the question

Former Prime Minister Paul Keating propelled the republic into the consciousness of the nation in the 1993 federal election. He launched the republic in his Bankstown policy speech, proposing that Australian people vote in a referendum to decide whether Australia should become a republic by 2001, the centenary of Federation.[1] This was a very significant promise made by a political leader to the electorate, and it was a promise with real appeal. According to Don Watson, Paul Keating's biographer and speechwriter, it was 'the grand moment of the speech': '[t]he applause was deafening and sustained. "It's time," he repeated over the din. At the end they were exultant ... [t]hey cheered Paul Keating to the rafters'.[2]

For eons leaders have used speeches, conventions and summits to develop and broadcast their ideas, and to engage the public in the debate. History also shows that the means used to put ideas into public consciousness may launch or sink a proposal. The story of republican reform is no different, as we can see by exploring the views of political leaders of the day, their proposals and their impact on public opinion.

There is a number of what might loosely be described as turning points in the Australian republican debate. These include:

- the republic becoming a political policy for the Labor and Liberal parties
- people moving from debating 'if' we should have a republic to 'what type' of republic
- political support for a republic waxing and waning.

These turning points were not so much a revolution as an evolution in republican consciousness in Australian politics.

Leaders: the catalysts for change

Of special importance was the role of the political leaders: Keating, Howard and Rudd. Public opinion changed in the early 1990s in favour of a republic,[3] a change that commentators have suggested was much to do with political and opinion leaders of the time, including Prime Minister Paul Keating.[4]

Prime Minister Paul Keating

Prime Minister Keating's first contribution to the debate was raising the question of the republic in the early 1990s, and subsequently making it an election promise and enshrining it in Labor Party policy. Essentially, Keating's vision was to maintain the current system of representative government but to replace the Queen with an Australian head of state.

In April 1993, Keating commissioned a Republic Advisory Committee to report on the minimum constitutional changes required to bring about a republic.[5] His response to their 1995 report, laid out in Parliament as a 'point by point ... precise proposal', indicated his preference for a model that would involve minimal change to the Australian Constitution.[6] The strength of the model was that it would 'please commonsense and feasibility'.[7] But it was not, and this was its weakness, a proposal designed specifically to engage the people in the process of change itself.

Don Watson summed up its mixed impact on public opinion: 'We launched the republic and immediately it was becalmed'; it was 'not sinking, but not sailing either'.[8] Prime Minister Keating responded to the mood of the people, endeavouring to engage them with a subsequent proposal: a plebiscite asking them whether they wanted Australia to become a republic.[9] Keating never got the opportunity to put his proposal to the Australian people as he lost the 1996 federal election.[10] Subsequent Australian Prime Ministers John Howard and more recently Kevin Rudd have also played important roles in influencing public debate.

Prime Minister John Howard

The question of the republic was a live issue in the 1996 election campaign, one that all party hopefuls had to consider and address. John Howard, the conservative Opposition Leader who won that election, sought to counter Keating's proposal of putting the question directly to the people in a referendum. Despite being a staunch monarchist, Howard saw that the momentum of public opinion was building in favour of a republic, so he proposed holding a constitutional convention as a means of addressing the issue, and this became an important part of Liberal Party policy.[11] This course of action was perceived by political commentators as successful precisely because Howard was seeking to engage the people in a consultative process, in turn bolstering his electoral popularity.[12] Interestingly, it was Howard, rather than Keating, who was then seen as the man in touch with the public's mood.[13]

The Constitutional Convention was held between 2 and 13 February 1998. It endorsed the suggestion of a Parliament-elected head of state and proposed that the model would be put to the people in a referendum in 1999. If successful, changes would be implemented in 2001.[14] The Convention was very successful at engaging people in the debate, particularly due to the fact that half the delegates were elected and represented many diverse groups, including the Australian Monarchist League, the Australian Republican Movement, Women for a Just Republic, the Greens, Bill of Rights supporters, Indigenous peoples, the Voice of Ordinary Fair-Minded Thinking Citizens and – my favourite – An Open Mind for the Future.[15] The debates themselves were seen as a success for democratic politics. The Convention also gave rise to community forums, such as the Women's Constitutional Convention.[16]

Mostly, the debate was intelligent, good-natured and vital,[17] but, ultimately, the Convention debates and resolutions had a negative impact. Kerry Jones, an elected delegate and Executive Director of Australians for Constitutional Monarchy, observed that the Convention was not about the Australian Republican Movement versus Australians for Constitutional Monarchy. Instead, 'The Convention pitted republicans against republicans and we were happy to get ready to observe the fireworks'.[18] The disagreement between republicans was compounded by the composition of the Convention. Half of the delegates were parliamentary representatives and persons appointed by the government, who mainly supported conservative changes.[19] Many of the republicans who favoured direct election were alienated by this process, and advocated a 'No' vote at the subsequent referendum.

However, there were signs of a deeper commitment to republicanism and of the likelihood of future successful constitutional reform. By the time of the referendum in 1999, there had been a significant shift in public debate. No longer were Australians debating *if* we should become a republic; rather, the debate was about what kind of republic we should become. Indeed, there was no reference to the Queen in the official literature provided to all eligible voters before the referendum![20]

The fate of the Queen then depended on the procedure for amending the Constitution. Under section 128 of the Australian Constitution, any amendments to the Constitution require a Bill to be passed by the Federal Parliament and then approved by a majority of voters in a majority of States.[21] On 6 November 1999, the Australian people were asked to vote 'Yes' or 'No' to:

> A PROPOSED LAW: To alter the Constitution to establish the Commonwealth of Australia as a republic with the Queen and Governor-General being replaced by a President appointed by a two-thirds majority of the members of the Commonwealth Parliament.

A total 44.74 per cent of people voted 'Yes' while 54.4 per cent voted 'No'.[22] The informal vote was less than 1 per cent, a very low figure, perhaps indicating that Australians were keen to have their say. However, the proposal was not carried nationally or in any State.

John Howard's response to the Convention's selected model no doubt contributed to its failure: for much of the debate he remained neutral, but in the dying days of the campaign he opposed it. Howard's critics have been harsh in their condemnation. Malcolm Turnbull, for instance, knew exactly who he felt was to blame when the referendum was lost: 'History will remember him for only one thing. He was the Prime Minister who broke the nation's heart.'[23] John Howard, though, believed he had an entitlement to put his own view, and that the people were entitled to know his opinion.[24] Ideally, the republican cause may have benefited by having two prominent political champions: the Leader of the Opposition and the Prime Minister. But the Convention ended up dividing rather than uniting the people in support of the republic. To paraphrase Abraham Lincoln, a house divided against itself cannot stand. The model could not win when it had less than complete bipartisan support at the time it was finally put to the people.

In 2000, after the defeat of the republic proposal, it must be noted – with some irony – that the Queen visited her loyal Australian subjects!

With the defeat of the republican referendum and Howard's preference to retain the status quo, the proposal for Australia to become a republic was taken off the political agenda of the government,[25] and the idea of Australia becoming a republic entered its wilderness years. Yet republican leaders remained faithful to the cause, trying to put the republic back on the nation's political agenda. Mostly they devoted their time and energy to finding new ways to engage people in republican reform. Two efforts stand out.

In December 2001, Richard McGarvie, a former Governor of Victoria, organised the People's Conference in Corowa, a NSW border town on the Murray River. The conference was inspired by the Corowa Conference of 1893, where the movement for Federation was restarted. One recommendation of the 2001 Corowa Conference was to establish all party parliamentary committees to achieve an early resolution of the head of state issue.[26]

In 2004, a bipartisan committee of the Senate published its report *The Road to a Republic*, which proposed a process for constitutional change that would include several plebiscites and a convention of constitutional experts to draft the changes needed.[27] Despite these efforts, John Howard's government never again officially engaged with the issue.

Prime Minister Kevin Rudd

The idea of a republic was once again revived with the election of the Rudd Government in November 2007. At the Rudd Government's 2020 Summit in April 2008, there was strong support for a multi-stage process for Australia to become a republic: a plebiscite on the issue, followed by widespread consultation, and finally, a referendum.[28] Kevin Rudd remarked that this support for the republic was 'a big step forward'.[29]

The Summit was significant because it was a consultative process designed to build consensus for change and, most importantly, help set a new political agenda for the nation. Prime Minister Rudd's consensus-based approach is quite a contrast to the more contentious republican politics of the Keating and Howard years.

Despite good intentions, the government provided a limited response to the 2020 Summit proposals in April 2009, highlighting that many of its current activities were directly related to the ideas put forward by the Summit as well as to make a commitment to nine practical new initiatives out of the more than 900 ideas generated.[30] In fact, the republican recommendation was not one of these initiatives. Once again, the political mood had changed and since the 2020 Summit the government has had to address the fallout from the global financial crisis.[31] Mr Rudd has indicated that the republic is not yet a priority but reaffirmed that Australians will be asked if they want to become a republic in a referendum.[32]

Perhaps the current state of public opinion can be used as a measure of the voters' likely support for an Australian republic. In May 2008, when asked in an opinion poll the question 'Should Australia become a republic with an elected president?', 45 per cent said 'Yes', 42 per cent said 'No' and 13 per cent were 'Undecided'.[33] To the question 'If Prince Charles were to be crowned King, in your opinion should Australia remain a monarchy, or become a republic with an elected president?' the figures changed: 56 per cent were for a republic, 32 per cent were for a monarchy and 11 per cent were undecided. And in a Nielsen poll conducted in September 2008, a majority (52 per cent) believed Australia should become a republic.[34] The same number supported the government giving a vote on Australia becoming a republic in the next couple of years.[35] Hope for the Australian republic, it seems, springs eternal.

The idea of Australia becoming a republic has now been embraced as part of mainstream politics. As we have seen, the public interest in this issue is significantly influenced by the means the country's political leaders use to engage them, but important questions remain concerning the most appropriate means. Whether a speech, convention or summit is used, this is but one issue in the shift towards adopting a republican form of government. In the next chapter, we consider the key constitutional steps by which the people may choose to become a republic. As we shall see, the Constitution leaves the ultimate decision with the people and their political leaders.

3

Altering the Australian Constitution

How do constitutional monarchies become republics? To answer this question let us look to history as our guide. In the eighteenth century, monarchies were overthrown through violent revolution. In France, for instance, the Kings and Queens were dragged off to the guillotine and publicly executed.[1] In the United States, colonial shackles were thrown off through a war of independence, and subsequently the founders drafted a federal Constitution.[2]

In the nineteenth century, Australian colonies established their nation state not through a war, but through a vote. By contrast to the revolutions that occurred in France and the United States, the development of Australian independence took an evolutionary route. It was envisaged by some framers of the Constitution that Australia would one day become a fully independent nation state. The framers also believed that from time to time the Constitution would need to be altered, and they provided a mechanism to amend it where any change would require an appeal to the people themselves. In the twenty-first century, if Australia is to become a republic, our Constitution requires that the proposal be approved by voters in a referendum.

From our history, we can identify six key political and legal steps required for constitutional change:

1. Putting the issue on the agenda
2. Developing the policy process
3. Selecting the model
4. Choosing the question
5. Informing the people
6. Altering the Constitution.

An initial examination of the key steps for choosing a republic will focus on the process of change rather than the aspects of various models. We will consider these models when we come to examine the constitutional design of a new head of state.

Chapter 2 examined how constitutional reform proposals are put into the public consciousness through the democratic process: speeches, conventions and conferences. In this context, we were examining the means chosen and their impact on public opinion.

Now, in this chapter, that history is revisited from a different perspective, to examine the key steps from the standpoint of the leaders, Parliament and constitutional amendment.

While constitutional lawyers have tended not to see constitutional change in this way,[3] section 128 of the Constitution necessarily requires a political process for change.[4] The change process involves: political leaders 'as sponsors of constitutional change',[5] Parliament framing the question, and the people as participants and decision makers. To explain the significance of this political process this analysis draws upon the views of the leaders themselves.

The six steps listed above seem clear enough, but their application is more complicated. For instance, in relation to step two, the development of a republican model by the political leaders will inevitably involve engagement with the public. Representatives, political parties, popular movements and individuals will all play a role in developing the appropriate solution. Moreover, the structure of a federal system means that national and State legislatures provide multiple forums for consideration and debate of the issue. Reform proposals will, therefore, be vigorously contested and debated.

While the steps have been outlined in chronological order, it is worth bearing in mind that the constitutional amending procedure frames the other steps, and should be addressed first.

Altering the Constitution

For a republic to be established in Australia, the amending procedure of the Australian Constitution in section 128 must be followed.[6] This amending process is a series of steps intended to bring about change, and typically adheres to the following procedure:

- A referendum Bill may be initiated in either House of the Federal Parliament.
- The Bill must be passed by an absolute majority in each House.
- The Bill must be submitted to the people, not less than two nor more than six months after its passage.[7]
- The Governor-General must exercise his or her discretion to put the Bill to a vote.
- A majority of voters in a majority of States must approve the proposed amendment.[8]
- Once the amending requirements of the Constitution have been fulfilled, the Bill is presented to the Governor-General to become law.

The Australian Constitution also provides an alternative procedure to resolve disagreements between the Houses of the Federal Parliament, allowing the lower House of Parliament to pass an amendment to the Constitution even where it has not received the approval of the Senate.[9]

But it would be incorrect to view section 128 as

simply a procedural provision, a mechanical set of steps that must be taken to achieve change. Rather, it refers to a series of interacting constitutional and democratic principles.[10] Principles are the vital ideas that inform our understanding of the rules in section 128, and representative democracy is one key principle. Ordinary parliamentary procedures mean that members may refer the Bill to committee for scrutiny, participate in debate and vote for the amendment Bill (in accordance with the procedure in section 128).

The choice of parliamentary representatives is constrained by the principle of responsible government.[11] The government that has the majority of seats in the House controls the initiation and voting for the amendment Bill. The Bill is then developed by the Attorney-General, Prime Minister and Cabinet. Once the Bill is passed by Parliament, the government can choose whether to put the proposal to the people. While either the Senate or the House of Representatives may pass a proposal, the Governor-General may only put it to the people on the advice of the Prime Minister. Thus, a Prime Minister might advise the Governor-General not to put a proposed amendment passed by the Senate to the people.

Federalism is another foundational principle for constitutional amendment, but it is not as prominent a limit. While members of the Senate are elected in Australia, the Senate's powers under section 128 are subordinated to that of the government in the lower

House. Also, the requirement in Australia that a majority of voters in a majority of States approve the amendment has impeded constitutional change in three out of 44 referenda. In other words, although a majority of voters nationwide approved a constitutional change, a majority of States did not.

The principle of parliamentary democracy is limited in Australia by the requirement of a referendum: the Parliament must pass legislation which is referred for final approval to a vote by the electorate. Accordingly, it is the people who enjoy the power of constitutional amendment.[12] As Professor Harrison Moore noted, if the people 'share the power with the Houses of the Parliament it is as predominant partners'.[13]

Later writers have seen other 'essential themes in constitutional alteration' such as 'participatory democracy and the sovereignty of the people'.[14] Thus, the amending procedure embodies referendum democracy, and is also characterised by a conservative voting formula. In the Australian context, while it has been easy enough to pass an amending proposal through the Federal Parliament, only a small number of referendums have been successful. The procedure imposes a high threshold as, by virtue of sheer numbers, it is more difficult to convince over half of Australia's voters than it is to convince half of its federal parliamentary members to support a constitutional change. Overall, popular and federal legitimacy are embodied in the referendum procedure.[15]

Putting the issue on the agenda

Before the amendment process can start, it is necessary for political or opinion leaders to put the issue on the national agenda. Two possibilities exist: Prime Minister and Leader of the Opposition. A Prime Minister might raise the issue for nationalist reasons. An Opposition Leader might put the issue on the agenda if the government does not because of its popularity and significance. But such a decision might not always be straightforward.

Former Prime Minister Paul Keating explains the leader's role of initiating change in the context of the republic debate:

> The Republic didn't ... exist ... it had some sentiment but no momentum ... The political leader is utterly central to such a change. First, without the political leader ... it can't be proposed, and second it would not happen.[16]

But how does a Prime Minister, or anyone else for that matter, come to the realisation to raise a proposal? Consideration of the proposal may arise from a trigger issue, such as a realisation borne of nationalism impacting personally. For Prime Minister Paul Keating, for instance, the republic 'spoke its own name'[17] and the issue touched him personally. As a new member of Parliament, Keating would go to schools and hand out the Australian flag. Seeing the flag of the United Kingdom in the corner of the Australian flag made him 'wince every time [he] had to give it out'.[18] Malcolm Turnbull, too, reacted against giving too many English dignitaries the right to speak at the bicentennial celebrations, believing that Australia should have its own head of state.[19]

Three other concerns apart from personal motivations have apparently influenced leaders' decisions to place the issue on the national agenda: risk, political opportunity and public opinion. For Prime Minister Paul Keating, the decision involved a balance between risk and opportunity. He was initially hesitant about introducing the idea of a republic because he believed he had to take it on at his 'own political risk'.[20] 'The Labor Party establishment wanted to play the 1993 election safe with economic and social issues.'[21] But Keating saw the need to act boldly in order to achieve the following nationalist goals:

- '[That] our head of state should embody and represent Australia's values and traditions, Australia's experience and aspirations.'[22]
- '[That the] Aboriginal people would not be alienated from the monarchy which, as the Crown, dispossessed them of their land and property.'[23]
- Development of a new national identity in a regional context inspired 'by the first Intra-Regional strategic body for the Pacific, the APEC leaders' meeting.'[24]

Prime Minister John Howard, who has maintained that he was 'not and never will be a republican',[25] nonetheless kept the republic on the political agenda for different reasons: to keep an election promise and as a means of managing public opinion. It was Liberal Party policy that if they won the 1996 federal election they would have a constitutional convention. The policy was developed by Alexander Downer and adopted by Howard when he became leader.

Howard wanted to keep faith with that clear pledge and saw the Constitutional Convention as a skilful way of handling the issue:

> There was some ... strong populist thought that Keating was advocating and ... the Liberal Party that was still predominantly anti-Republican [must] have a device ... that allowed for debate but preserved their own position.[26]

Thus, John Howard recognised the right of the community and his own party to air their views.[27] But as he saw it, issues once raised may also be removed from public consideration. For John Howard: '[t]he process for examining it [had] been exhausted and the people have spoken'. He took the issue off the political agenda, stating emphatically that: 'I don't think there is a prospect of this country ever becoming a republic while this monarch lives ... people have said no and ... that's it.'[28]

With the failure of the 1999 referendum, the question of a republic lost its prominence as a political issue. This is not to say, however, that it did not have considerable support amongst Australian politicians.

In 2004, the Senate report, *The Road to a Republic*,[29] was written by a bipartisan committee and provided a road map for republic reform. Kim Beazley, as Leader of the national Opposition, thought differently to John Howard. He said the choice for voters in the 2004 election was between 'a party that's prepared to put the issue before them and a party that won't'.[30]

In 2007 Kevin Rudd won the federal election and the republic re-emerged as a political issue. The Prime Minister has been influenced by Labor Party policy and the need to manage public opinion. In a radio interview Kevin Rudd commented that, 'I'm a longstanding republican, and we're committed as a party to bring about a republic ... We lost the last referendum nearly ten years ago, we don't want to lose the next one. So we'll be building this one up very carefully'. He also said that 'you do need widespread community support ... A republican referendum will only be successful on a bipartisan basis.[31]

But public opinion has a haunting legacy – failure. Failure has made our political leaders timid and cautious, and that legacy apparently looms large in the minds of Kevin Rudd and Malcolm Turnbull. Rudd's overtures of seeking bipartisan support on Malcolm Turnbull's first day of becoming Opposition Leader were resisted.[32] Malcolm Turnbull said, when he became Leader of the Liberal Party: 'I don't want to use the republican issue for political advantage, having another referendum and losing it – that does nobody any good.'[33] Professor John Warhurst believes that '[each] of them has to develop their own approach, independent of the other, before bringing it to the common table'.[34] In light of these various factors, we await the Prime Minister's and Malcolm Turnbull's response in the near future.

Importantly, it is not only political leaders who have played a role in putting the republic issue on the agenda. It is also notable that groups like the Australian Republican Movement, a voluntary organisation, have been tireless in their efforts to obtain regular publicity for the central message of the desirability of a republic.

Developing the policy process

For a republic to be established, leaders will need to develop a policy process and a republican model will need to be chosen to replace the current system of constitutional monarchy. To this point, various policy processes have been adopted by Australia's representatives to develop a model: Prime Minister Keating commissioned a panel of experts, Prime Minister Howard created a constitutional convention, the Senate Committee inquiry published a report, and Prime Minister Rudd held his 2020 Summit. The establishment of advisory committees, conventions and summits ultimately derive their authority from the Prime Minister. However, Prime Ministers are prepared 'to let [committees] talk their way through the issues and recommend proposals and changes ...'.[35] This is perhaps based on a view that the people must have a role in development of proposals; and that the way policy is developed is influenced by the constitutional amending procedures. The constitutional requirements of representative and referendum democracy ensure that the choice of the model rests not only with the representatives but with the people themselves. Thus the policy needs to engage both political leaders and the people. But different visions of constitutional democracy influenced the political leaders' development of their proposal. Prime Minister Keating commissioned a Republic Advisory Committee to:[36]

- examine the complex constitutional issues involved
- describe the necessary constitutional changes to create a republic
- consult widely
- be bipartisan.[37]

For Paul Keating, the Republic Advisory Committee was a 'proponent for change' – bipartisan and composed of republicans working together to develop a model. This model would then be debated and voted on at a referendum.

Howard's idea was that the republic and the republican model could only happen through debate and discussion. Prime Minister Howard held the Constitutional Convention because it was 'the normal thing to do'.[38] The Convention was designed to 'debate this issue' and allow 'greater involvement of the people in the whole issue and in formulating the question'.[39] In 1995 he believed it was the 'best vehicle' to unite Australians on the republic issue.[40] In an interview Howard clarified the meaning of the word 'unite' as:

> ... a fairly creative use of the word but, united in the sense that they felt that they have their say, in the sense that a democratic election does unite people. Although they are unhappy or half the population is unhappy with the outcome, they don't feel disenfranchised.[41]

John Howard saw Keating's Republic Advisory Committee as 'a stacked deck', because all the members were republicans. Although he:

> couldn't say it at the time because all of the committee were reputable people entitled to their point of views ... My argument was let's debate this issue but let's have this convention that would allow people to be more heavily involved.[42]

Malcolm Turnbull, though, saw Howard's Constitutional Convention as an obstacle to republican change, 'with no common purpose', a convention 'calculated to highlight disagreements between republicans' with at least 'a third of its members determined to retain the status quo'.[43]

The 2004 Senate Committee inquiry published *The Road to a Republic*, emphasising direct democracy. Significantly, the Senate's report helped shift the focus of reform from constitutional conventions and parliamentary forums to plebiscites of the people. The Senate report articulated a four-stage process: an initial plebiscite asking Australians whether Australia should become a republic;[44] a subsequent plebiscite asking them which of a variety of models they would prefer;[45] a convention of constitutional experts to fine-tune the model;[46] and finally, submission of the model through Parliament to the people via a referendum to amend the Australian Constitution.[47]

Kevin Rudd's 2020 Summit shifted the focus away from plebiscites on the kind of model that should be adopted to the question itself: 'Should Australia become a republic?' It envisioned widespread community consultation and then a referendum. Finally, the Senate has again taken the lead in advancing the cause of the republic. It is currently considering an Act to require a plebiscite on whether Australia should become a republic at the next federal election.[48]

Whether the Senate's plebiscite program (for development of the model) will be adopted may depend upon the views of federal parliamentarians themselves. Some parliamentarians like Liberal Senator Mitch Fifield argue that the proper place for the development of the model is through the Parliament itself, not through plebiscites. Others, like Member of Parliament Nicola Roxon, argue that the plebiscite process is vital to the success of any proposed amendment, because any proposal must gain majority support of the Australian citizens at a referendum to amend the Australian Constitution.[49]

Selecting the model

Once the consultative process has been developed a model must be chosen. Professor Greg Craven has remarked: 'It is often said everybody has at least one novel in them; it seems that every Australian has at least one model for a republic.'[50] Craven's comment is not only humorous, it's also poignant – there may be as many models as there are Australians. But only one model can ultimately be adopted. We must therefore narrow our choices. The various proposals and options which have found favour typically address five criteria:

1. A new office of head of state is established and given a title, such as President. The qualifications or eligibility for the office are specified.

2. The procedure for the appointment and removal of the head of state are prescribed.

3. Presidential powers or functions are identified and limited.

4. The implication of a republic for the States is considered.

5. Rewriting of the Constitution is necessary.

Successful options need to be justifiable, functional and viable. Each of the five criteria must be justifiably addressed, and to ensure functionality the model must provide a reasonable accommodation of the criteria. To be viable it must gain official recognition and be put to the people by the political leaders, since the Parliament is the only body that may enact the referendum Bill.

Three official proposals will now be considered. It is likely that one of these would be put to the people, and indeed one already has. Each of the three official proposals assumes that the President would have the same powers and functions as the Governor-General.

The Keating model

Paul Keating's model ushered in the term 'President' for the new office of head of state, a role that can be compared to the office of Governor-General. In many ways, the Keating proposal laid the foundation for subsequent models. His criteria for head of state were:

Eligibility

All candidates would be Australian citizens of voting age. Formal procedures would be put in place to ensure that the new office would be open to all citizens. Under the current system, no qualifications for the Governor-General are provided in the Constitution.

Appointment and removal

A single nomination would be made by the Prime

Minister; election and dismissal would be conducted by a two-thirds majority vote in a joint sitting of the Commonwealth Parliament. The grounds for removal would be incapacity or guilt of proven misbehaviour. The two-thirds majority procedure would make it 'impossible for any government to dictate the outcome of this process'.[51] Under the current arrangements, the Governor-General is appointed and removed by the Queen acting on the advice of the Prime Minister.

Presidential powers or functions

The President's powers would remain the same as those of the Governor-General. This would enable the head of state to resolve a constitutional crisis. To provide a check against a President who might be tempted to abuse his or her position of power, there would be enacted new constitutional provisions recognising continuity of the constitutional conventions, although the Constitution would not specify their content. Thus, the powers of the head of state would be incorporated by reference to their inheritance in current practice.[52]

Republic and the States

The States would be constitutional monarchies with the Queen as head of state. Her representative in each State is the Governor. Each State would be free to choose for itself whether it remains a monarchy.[53]

Rewriting the Constitution

Apart from the above amendments, other changes would be largely incidental, often simply replacing references to the Crown, Queen, or Governor-General with the appropriate republican term, without altering the practical effect of the provisions.

The 1999 referendum model

The 1999 referendum model was similar to the Keating model in that:[54]

- eligibility for office was to be an Australian citizen, qualified to be a member of the House of Representatives[55]
- the term of office was to be five years, but unlike the Keating proposal more than one term was possible
- the powers of the President were defined by reference to constitutional conventions.

The significance of the 1999 referendum model was the introduction of a nominations committee and the alteration to the appointment and removal procedure.

Nomination

A single nomination would be made by the Prime Minister after consideration of a report of a 32-person committee composed of federal parliamentary representatives of all parties, State representatives and community members. The purpose of the committee was to receive nominations and to propose candidates of diverse backgrounds but with outstanding ability.

Appointment procedure

Appointment would be moved by the Prime Minister, seconded by the Leader of the Opposition and approved by a two-thirds majority of a joint sitting of Commonwealth Parliament. Unlike the Keating proposal, a role would be provided for the Leader of the Opposition, providing explicit bipartisan support for the candidate.

Dismissal of the President

The head of state would be dismissed by the Prime Minister, subject to approval by the House of Representatives. This dismissal procedure was meant to be similar to the current dismissal procedure for the Governor-General.

With the failure of the 1999 referendum model, the possibility for alternate models was opened up to debate.

The Senate report

The report *The Road to a Republic* suggested five alternative methods for appointing the head of state:[56]

1. Prime Ministerial appointment
2. Appointment by a two-thirds majority of a joint sitting of Parliament
3. Appointment by an electoral college
4. Direct election of Parliament's candidates

5   Direct election by the people

Prime ministerial appointment, the first suggested method, would be similar to the status quo, while the second method (appointment by a two-thirds majority of a joint sitting of Parliament) would be similar to the model presented at the 1999 referendum. The third model adopts an electoral college, comprising an equal number of elected members from each State, along the lines currently provided for in the Senate. The college would appoint the President, from persons who had obtained at least 1000 nominations, of which at least one hundred must be from each State.

In the direct election models, it was proposed to codify or specify the powers of the head of state. This was due to the expectation that an election would give a head of state a popular mandate which requires the specification of explicit powers to maintain the current non-executive role of the head of state.

The Senate's report is significant because it illustrates the changed focus of the debate from proposals to options. The report didn't propose one model but multiple models for community discussion and decision. As Professor George Williams has remarked, 'almost any model is potentially [constitutionally] achievable'.[57] This comment raises issues of constitutional design, which will be addressed in chapters 5, 6 and 7. Of course selecting a model is one thing. Choosing the question to be put to the people is another thing altogether.

Choosing the question

Once the model has been developed and selected, Parliament has responsibility for phrasing the question. The question put to the people in a referendum is the long title of the amendment Bill. The form of the question is specified by legislation in a two-step process: (1) voters are asked about the proposal to alter the Constitution, and (2) the voter is asked to approve of the proposed law.[58]

We can learn much about asking the question from the way it was hotly contested in the 1999 referendum. In this instance there were three formulations of the proposal: the initial Bill, a joint parliamentary committee and the final version (favoured by John Howard). The wording of the proposal in the original Bill was:

> The Constitution should be altered to establish the Commonwealth of Australia as a Republic with a president chosen by a two-thirds majority of Parliament. [59]

The wording of the proposal by the Joint Select Committee was:

> A Bill for an Act to alter the Constitution to establish the Commonwealth of Australia as a republic, with the Queen and Governor-General being replaced by an Australian President.[60]

The final proposal put to the people was:

> A proposed law: To alter the Constitution to

establish the Commonwealth of Australia as a republic with the Queen and Governor-General being replaced by a President appointed by a two-thirds majority of the members of the Commonwealth Parliament.

The original bill

John Howard commented on the original question, saying he felt 'it was an accurate summary' of the proposed change.[61] Kim Beazley, on the other hand, expressed his concern, saying that: '... a question put that way is almost invariably going to fail ...' unless the people were properly consulted.[62]

The response of each leader is suggestive of typical oppositional politics. However, the deeper issue here, and one raised by the debate, is that the form of the question may structure its response: if you ask the right question, will you receive the right answer? In addition, this wasn't simply a party political dispute; differences emerged between monarchists and republicans. Even so, there was bipartisan support for a new question.

The Committee proposal

The Joint Select Committee, consisting of equal numbers of government and opposition members from each House, was established to review the original Bill. The decision of the Committee was unanimous.[63] The Committee explained its reasons for its choice of question:

> ... the Committee received many suggestions about the appropriate content of the long title. These suggestions addressed issues ranging from the replacement of the Queen and Governor-General with a President, the powers of the President, and the selection and the dismissal of the President, all of which are dealt with in the Republic Bill. To list each of them would be to create a very long, complex and unreadable long title. To mention only one, however, might give undue emphasis to that aspect. The Committee therefore prefers amendments to the long title of the Republic Bill that would avoid such complexity
>
> ...
>
> The Committee concludes that the most appropriate long title for the Republic Bill would be one that presents clearly and simply the essential purpose and outcome of the proposed legislation. The Committee recommends, therefore, that the Republic Bill's long title be amended to refer simply to the outcome of the amendments included in the Republic Bill.[64]

While the report explained the principles justifying the Committee's decision, Bob Charles, the Liberal Chair of the Committee, explained its politics:

> Those who wanted a monarchy wanted it as long and as complicated as possible in order to confuse people so they wouldn't vote for it. Those who wanted a republic wanted it as simple and straightforward as possible. We wanted to walk a fine line in [the] committee and we discussed it for a long time.[65]

Kim Beazley said it was 'clearly the only version which had much of a show'[66] while John Howard felt it was 'loading' the question. He thought it was asking 'if you really want to vote for an Australian or not ...' and he expected that 'Everybody would vote for an Australian'.[67] For John Howard, asking the question in this way was like asking 'whether you want a pay rise'![68] The Prime Minister, therefore, wanted to change the question.

The final proposal

John Howard 'wanted ... a question that was neutral on the subject of Australian nationalism ... We just took out the words 'Australian' because the Governor-General is Australian'.[69] His approach was that:

> ... the referendum question should be as succinct as possible and it should have the essence of the proposal ... that ... was threefold. Firstly, that the Commonwealth of Australia should be established as a republic, and ... that the Queen ... and Governor-General ... should be replaced by a President chosen by two-thirds majority of Parliament. ... that was just a statement of the essential facts, without any attendant swear words or colour.[70]

Bob Charles remarked that 'We were pretty happy with it, basically. [The Committee] would probably have preferred that the method of selection hadn't appeared but you could never say it wasn't fair to have it appear ...'[71] Kim Beazley commented that he would have preferred not to have the Queen and Governor-

General in the question because 'she's very popular'.⁷²

Robert McClelland, a Labor member of the Joint Select Committee, believed that the final question 'consider[ed] one part of the process only'. According to McClelland the question ignored 'community involvement in the nomination process, a joint nomination by the Prime Minister and Leader of the Opposition ... [and] parliamentary approval.'⁷³

Thus, the political leaders disagreed as to the fairness of the question and its popular appeal.

Given these differing views, how might the question have influenced the voters' decision? As it happens, an *Age*/AC Nielsen Poll was taken at the time comparing voters' support for the final question (Mr Howard's question) and the Committee's question. Here is what it found:

> The referendum question is likely to be defeated if [Howard's] existing question was put but was likely to succeed if the committee question was put. Thirty-one per cent of respondents would support Mr Howard's wording with 55 per cent against, in contrast 57 per cent supported the committee's wording with 33 per cent against.⁷⁴

Should public opinion inform the formulation of a referendum question? Once again, the four leaders – Howard, Beazley, Charles and McClelland – all had different points of view on this matter.

John Howard said, 'I really can't answer that. I don't incidentally think that the precise wording in the question had an enormous amount to do with how people think, it may have influenced some people but I don't think it influenced too many people in the end'.[75] Kim Beazley felt that no political leader can 'study the polls without understanding how dramatically things ... change in ... alleged public opinion when the question is changed. Questions are important, the way they're formulated is critical ... but [Howard] understood that the ways in [which] questions are asked are critical'.[76] Robert McClelland agreed and believed that the phrasing of the question will make it very very difficult for the referendum to succeed.[77] By contrast, Bob Charles doubted the reliability of the poll and said: 'I'm not confident that the wording of the referendum determined the outcome at all.'[78]

It is important to note that each political leader was commenting on the final question. What is clear is that the leaders don't think that the debate over the question is simply nitpicking, each acknowledging that the phrasing of the question could influence the answer.

What was unusual about this republican referendum is that we have opinion poll evidence on two questions, indicating that the wording of the question can certainly affect the answer, supporting Kim Beazley and Rob McClelland's views. When comparing the outcome of the vote in the republic referendum with this earlier opinion poll evidence, the difference suggests that the republicans were effective in their campaign. Initial support for the Howard question was 31 per cent but at the referendum 46 per cent of people voted for the republic.

Two further points can be made about opinion poll evidence. First, the opinion poll evidence is only current for the day the question is asked. Second, people's views about a topic may change significantly after an election campaign. Neither Howard nor Charles were confident that the wording of the question determined the outcome. Other factors such as information provided to the voters and the referendum campaign apparently had an impact too.

Informing the people

The final step to be examined in the process of choosing a republic is that the people must be informed and convinced to support the proposed republican model. In this, the 1999 referendum was quite different from previous referendums.

Previous Campaigns

In the past, a referendum usually involved a campaign between a supporting government and an opposition who disapproved of the amendment. In this context, legislation was enacted to guarantee a 'fairly' informed campaign where two measures have been crucial: provision of information and a ban on Commonwealth funding.

An official 'Yes' and 'No' case (prepared by members

of Parliament who support or oppose the referendum Bill) as well as textual changes to the Constitution, are distributed in a pamphlet to electors.[79] If members of Parliament do not oppose the referendum there will only be a Yes case. The Yes/No pamphlet was introduced in 1912, to ensure each case was presented 'in an impersonal, reasonable and judicial way ... rather than [appealing] to the emotions and party sentiments'.[80]

The sentiment behind the proposal is captured in the words of the then Labor Prime Minister, Mr Fisher. He remarked: 'the case will be put from both sides impersonally ... Let it be a document that the Parliament will be proud of, from which Australia will benefit'.[81]

Unfortunately, the pamphlet has not lived up to its lofty goals. Commentators have been critical of the pamphlet as being increasingly unsatisfactory. Professor Saunders has remarked that '[t]he aim of ... the cases [are] no longer to inform, rather, each side prepares its case with a view to winning, apparently on any ground',[82] and that 'the emergence of the electronic media' means that less attention will be paid to 'the drab official referendum pamphlet'.[83]

In addition, legislation requires that no other public monies may be spent by the Commonwealth Government advocating either case.[84] This requirement was designed to prevent additional Commonwealth funds from being used in a partisan fashion by the government of the day to promote one side of the debate (usually the Yes case). However, the States are not prevented from spending funds to run their own referendum campaigns.

The 1999 referendum campaign

By 1999, the publication of only a Yes/No case did not seem to fit the realities of modern media communications and there was pressure for public funding of information and advertising. Important changes to legislation were introduced providing public funding for an information campaign and to support advertising for the Yes/No case.[85] The politics of the 1999 referendum were also distinctive. The Labor Party supported the referendum, the Liberal government allowed a conscience vote and their coalition partners the Nationals opposed it. John Howard and senior members of his Cabinet opposed the referendum too.

So, a further change to the legislation was made. The Yes/No committees were composed of community representatives drawn from the Constitutional Convention – not the usual parliamentarians. The official reason for appointing Constitutional Convention delegates to the committees was to provide better community representation and to elevate the debate above party politics.[86] However, some may infer that this conveniently enabled the Liberal government to distance itself from the debate, allowing its members freedom from party discipline.[87]

The federal government spent $19.5 million on the

referendum in two phases. The first $4.5 million was spent on an education program which sought to:[88]

- outline Australia's current constitutional system
- explain the proposed republican model put forward by the Constitutional Convention in February 1998
- explain the process for making any changes to Australia's Constitution and State constitutions.

The education campaign was developed after consultation with an impartial panel of experts.[89]

In the second phase the Howard government provided $7.5 million for each of the Yes and No committees.[90] This funding was for 'national advertising campaigns in the four-week period leading up to referendum day'.[91] The public funding was important as a means of educating and engaging the public, and without this funding it is unlikely that the Liberal Party would have spent money on the campaign because it held a conscience vote. In addition, questions would arise over whether other political parties would have spent money if this was the case.

Two criticisms have been made of the government's education campaign. Kim Beazley argued that:

> The public education campaign was inadequate in terms of fulfilling the desire ... for real information on the issues. The lack of detailed public awareness of ... [the] Constitution paved the way for the success of a scare campaign.[92]

David Freeman, writing in the *Public Law Review*, has argued:

> Although the composition of the committees may have increased the contribution of a select group of non-politicians ... the real problem is not who is involved in the public debate but how it is conducted. These committees only re-enforced the adversarial nature of constitutional reform rather than promoting reform by consensus, which would require a much longer information campaign ...[93]

Each criticism is supportive of a sustained education campaign in any future republican referendum. Freeman's reference to the 'adversarial nature' of the 1999 referendum campaign raises the question of the referendum's failure. Consideration given to the mechanisms for convincing the people also raises a question about the subject matter of the debates themselves. Each of these issues will be dealt with in chapter 8.

Conclusion

If you were only to read the text of section 128, the constitutional amendment procedure, you might think that the only important actors were the Parliament, the Governor-General and the people. This, as we have seen, is only part of the story. We must look beyond the words of the section to understand the political process which is necessarily required for constitutional amendment.

Several political principles are referred to in section 128. The most important one is responsible government, which vests the power of initiation, development of the proposal and choice of the model in the hands of the Prime Minister and Cabinet. Representative democracy is also vital. Parliament chooses the question and enacts the Bill containing the changes to the Constitution. Legislation is also important for it regulates the way in which referendum campaigns are run and prescribes how the people are to be informed. The legislation requires the people have an either/or choice to make the change. In either case, it is the will of the people that prevails. It follows then that section 128 describes the final steps in the process.

Section 128 outlines that the choice of the representatives and the people will be by majority decision – parliamentary, federal and popular – but what is not written is the content of the change itself. The substance of the debate is what enlivens the amending procedure. The approach taken by leaders and parliamentarians is very much influenced by their personal and political views and ambitions. Some motivations included influencing public opinion, developing a viable model, nationalism, framing the best question, and winning the campaign. Thus, it is democracy that animates section 128.

4

Glimpsing the Governor-General

'The best reason why monarchy is a strong government is that it is an intelligible government. The mass of mankind understand it, and they hardly anywhere in the world understand any other.'[1] So said Walter Bagehot, writing in his seminal work *The English Constitution* in 1872.

Bagehot believed in the strength of monarchy because people understood its basic idea – a society ruled by a king or queen. Constitutional monarchy was also an idea that he believed was generally intelligible, as most had a vague understanding that rules governed how the Queen acts and that there were other institutions of government.[2] However, Bagehot cautioned that there were 'whole classes unable to comprehend the idea of a constitution'.[3]

Today, the Queen's role is mostly as a ceremonial head of state. In Australia we see little of this ceremony, except perhaps for the Queen's Christmas message – if we still happen to be awake after Christmas lunch. More informally, we read about the exploits of her children in the tabloids or celebrity magazines. But despite this popular interest, any royal visit does bring genuine feelings of sentiment and, at times, pride.

Even before Bagehot wrote his text, the world had already changed. The American Revolution created a tectonic shift in politics, establishing in the Western psyche the pre-eminence of elected governments.[4] Today, democratic government is strong government because it is intelligible. As a population we understand democracy because it is played out through the media constantly – at a saturation level that brings news of the government directly into our living rooms, every day. We practise democracy in the vote and see the result of our choice in the Parliament – a government and an opposition, a diversity of parties and political groups. The Prime Minister, the Leader of the Opposition and other Ministers star in a political opera that is performed for the public 24/7.

Electors may not have a perfect understanding of politics or of constitutional law. We may hanker for co-operation and more consensus, but, in fact, the litmus test of parliamentary democracy is competing party elites, vigorous debate and opposition. At times the political opera may leave us with a cynical response towards events and at its players but despite this, Australians are generally not cynical about their democracy.[5]

By contrast to our perceptions of partisan politics, few of us appreciate or fully understand the role of the Governor-General, perhaps as, in comparison, we get only glimpses of the Governor-General's role via the media. Photo opportunities that present themselves for public consumption tend to be for ceremonial occasions. So what do we see of the Governor-General's role in the media? Swearing in the Ministers of State after an election, commissioning military officers and awarding honours and honouring the war dead. Also making important public statements, such as at times of natural disasters like floods and bush fires, and of course awarding the Melbourne Cup!

Sometimes the actions of the Governor-General come into the media spotlight, such as in the 1975 constitutional crisis or the coverage of the controversial events leading to Governor-General Hollingsworth's resignation in 2003. In order to fully understand the Governor-General's constitutional role it is important to go behind the scenes and explain some of her other functions.

The Constitution

Under our current political system, power is divided between the head of state – the Queen (whose representative in Australia is the Governor-General) – and the head of the elected government (the Prime Minister). These two significant roles operate in different ways. The Governor-General is appointed and removed by the Queen acting on the advice of the Prime Minister. The Governor-General has a variety of functions as a national leader, an office holder under the Constitution, and in performing ceremonial functions.

The Prime Minister, in comparison, leads the political party that gains the majority of seats in the House of Representatives, and bears ultimate responsibility to Parliament for all government actions. The Prime Minister is also responsible for developing the government's legislative program, having it approved by Parliament, and for formulating government policy and advising the head of state on formal matters.[6]

The Queen's representative

Some believe that the Governor-General is our head of state,[7] while others believe that he or she is the 'officiating' or 'constitutional' head of state.[8] Some see the Governor-General as the head of state for the Commonwealth, although not described officially in this way.[9] Sometimes these arguments rest on the constitutional independence of the office. In 1988 the Constitutional Commission commented on the status of the office:

> Although the Governor-General is the Queen's representative in Australia, the Governor-General is in no sense a delegate of the Queen. The

independence of the office is highlighted by changes which have been made in recent years to the Royal instruments relating to it.[10]

Despite the Governor-General's independence, there is conjecture, uncertainty and ambiguity about the status of the vice-regal office. The Governor-General's role in these circumstances is best understood in qualified terms. Whatever the merit of these qualified views, it is important to be clear about a vital fact: Australia has a Queen. The Constitution makes this abundantly clear. The Queen's representative is the Governor-General.

Which office holder then is at the apex of our constitutional system? Which person is designated as the chief public representative of our country? The status and position of the two offices, the Queen and her representative, are explicit and distinct in the Australian Constitution. The Constitutional Commission in 1988 regarded the Queen as the head of state because of the role it gives to her:

> She is a constituent part of the Federal Parliament (section 1) and the Governor-General assents to Bills passed by the two Houses of Parliament in her name (section 58). She appoints the Governor-General to be her representative in the Commonwealth and she alone may remove the Governor-General from office (section 2). The executive power of the Commonwealth is formally vested in the Queen, but is declared to be exercisable by the Governor-General (section 61). The persons

appointed to administer federal departments are declared to be "the Queen's Ministers of State for the Commonwealth" (section 64). The salaries payable from the Consolidated Revenue Fund to the Governor-General and the Ministers are formally payable to the Queen (sections 3 and 66).[11]

The Queen's status was recognised in 1953 by giving her the official title of Queen of Australia, in addition to also being the Queen of the United Kingdom.[12] While this was a step towards Australian independence from Great Britain, it also reinforced the position of the monarch in Australia's system of government. Since the Queen was always going to be physically absent, the Governor-General is recognised in the Constitution as the person who exercises the Queen's functions in Australia. When the Queen is personally present in Australia she may exercise some of the Governor-General's powers.[13] The position and role of the monarch in the Constitution identifies her as the head of state of Australia, and the Governor-General as the Queen's representative. Thus, it is right for republicans to say that the Queen is *the* head of state. The better description of the Governor-General is as her representative. But what does this role really entail?

Ceremony and leadership

The Governor-General's representative role is to act as a national leader, a figure of national unity. In fact, the office is able to be supported by all political parties,[14] because the Governor-General is not a member of any political party.[15] She does not take part in the business of partisan politics, removing the office from the antagonisms and disparagements of the political arena. However, the Governor-General does have the non-partisan political function 'to interpret the nation to itself'.[16] In this context the Governor-General's main power is to apolitically raise important national issues.[17] For instance, William Deane, who was Governor-General from 1999–2001, promoted humanitarian and liberal values in Indigenous affairs, and Quentin Bryce, the current Governor-General (2008–) has raised the issue of the plight of communities of the drought-affected Murray-Darling Basin.[18] Depending upon one's political point of view such stances may be seen either as exemplary vice-regal behaviour or as pushing the boundaries.[19]

In addition, the Governor-General presides at many ceremonies and awards and is a patron of many organisations. Attending these related functions are part of the Governor-General's office's function and take up considerable time. As former Governor-General, Sir Paul Hasluck remarked:

> Some involve ceremonial occasions arising from his place in Australian government – the opening of Parliament, the administering of oaths of office, the receiving of credentials from foreign ambassadors, the holding of investitures, the taking of parades,

the receiving of heads of state of other countries. Some involve public duties on behalf of national and international institutions and societies, such as the opening of conferences, attendance at major public gatherings, presentation of the awards and so on. As patron of many organisations, as Prior of the Order of St John, as Chief Scout and in similar capacities he has regular demands on his time.[20]

Even though the Governor-General spends significant time at ceremonies, the office still occupies an important constitutional position.

Elections and inauguration

The Governor-General presides over the inauguration of a government and the election of the Parliament. It is her responsibility to guarantee the smooth transition of power from one government to another, a role that is prescribed by the very terms of the Constitution itself. Thus the Constitution vests the office with the powers to:

- cause writs to be issued for a general House of Representatives election (section 32)
- issue writs for a by-election in the absence of the Speaker of the House (section 33)
- fix session times and prorogue Parliament (section 5)
- summon Parliament and dissolve the House of Representatives (section 5, 28)
- dissolve both Houses where there is a deadlock

between them and convene a joint sitting (section 57)
- establish departments of state (section 64)
- appoint and dismiss Ministers of State (section 64) and, in the absence of parliamentary provision, direct what offices Ministers shall hold (section 65).

These powers of the Governor-General as an authority to summon, dissolve, appoint, dismiss and issue writs are couched in the ancient language of Parliament and the law. But what do these various terms mean? The Governor-General commands Parliament to hold an election by issuing a writ – a written order. They have a discretion to fix the session times of Parliament, which are the sittings, when members take their seats to conduct the business of Parliament.[21] They summon Parliament to a meeting after a general election which begins the life of the Parliament,[22] preside at its formal opening,[23] and when Parliament is closed by a dissolution there must be a general election.[24] They prorogue Parliament which brings to an end the sittings: all business of Parliament is either set aside or annulled.[25] By contrast the President of the Senate and the Speaker of the House's call for an adjournment merely interrupts a sitting until they recall their respective Chamber.[26]

These are great powers that the Governor-General holds. However, such powers of controlling parliamentary proceedings gain little notoriety and are therefore rarely visible to the public. One notable exception occurred in 1975. On the steps of old Parliament House Sir David Smith performed his role as Secretary to the Governor-General, reading a proclamation calling for the 1975 general election,[27] much to the dismay of the recently dismissed Prime Minister Gough Whitlam.

The function we most often see in the media is the swearing in or inauguration ceremony. On this occasion the ministry is formally appointed as the government, each Minister swearing an oath or affirmation presided over by the Governor-General. The Governor-General traditionally opens Parliament after an election.[28] This takes on a far greater significance in Canada than in Australia, where the Governor-General reads out a speech prepared by the government. There is much fanfare about the speech 'from the Throne' in Parliament,[29] which is distinguished from the American ritual of the inaugural speech of an American President. Both the speech of the Governor-General of Canada and the United States President signals the beginning of a new government, when politics is once again renewed after an election.

Exercising the executive power of the Commonwealth

What obviously distinguishes Australian Government from that of the United States is the presence of the Queen and her representative, the Governor-General. This is made clear by the words of section 61 of the

Constitution, which reads:

> The executive power of the Commonwealth is vested in the Queen and is exercisable by the Governor-General as the Queen's representative, and extends to the execution and maintenance of this Constitution, and of the laws of the Commonwealth.

The term 'executive power' refers to the power to administer the law and to manage the government, especially government departments. The Governor-General is also vested by the Constitution with other executive functions, such as the power to:

- 'according to his discretion', assent to legislation passed by both Houses of Parliament (section 58)
- command the defence forces (section 68)
- appoint public servants (section 67)
- appoint, and remove upon an address from both Houses, judges of the High Court and of other federal courts (section 72)
- appoint members of the Interstate Commission[30] (section 103)
- submit a referendum proposal to the people where there is a deadlock between the two Houses (section 128).

After reading the provisions of the Constitution, it may seem that the Governor-General independently makes the decisions, but actually this is not the case.

Constitutional practice has long established that the Governor-General's exercise of the executive power of the Commonwealth is on the advice of the elected government.

Acting on advice

The obligation on the Governor-General to act on advice is mentioned occasionally in provisions that refer to the advice of the Federal Executive Council, a body comprised of the Governor-General and Ministers. These are important provisions because they recognise the principle of responsible government. Other constitutional provisions vest powers in the Governor-General alone, but this does not mean that he or she may act independently, since these sections of the Constitution do not mean quite what they say. This might sound extraordinary to a lay person, but constitutions are not interpreted in a vacuum. Rather, the words of the Constitution are understood against rules induced from political practice. These are traditions, not rules of law. They are non-justiciable[31] and are often described as constitutional conventions.[32] As John Quick and Robert Garran, two of the first commentators on the Australian Constitution, noted:

> Whilst, therefore, in this Constitution some executive powers are, in technical phraseology, and in accordance with venerable customs, vested in the Governor-General, and others in the Governor-General

in Council, they are all substantially in pari materia, on the same footing, and, in the ultimate resort, can only be exercised according to the will of the people.[33]

Thus the great powers of the Governor-General are exercised in accordance with the principle of responsible government: the Governor-General as an appointed official acts on the advice of the Ministers who are members of the party that commands a majority in the popularly elected House. Ministers are answerable to the Parliament and ultimately to the will of the people through regular elections. Ministers, not the Governor-General, bear ultimate political responsibility for the actions of the government.

However, in acting on advice, the Governor-General retains the power to counsel, advise and warn.[34] This in itself denies Ministers absolute power. In fact, 'the boundaries between ... exercising the "right to warn" and the refusal to comply with ministerial advice may not always be very clear'.[35] While these powers appear to be a built-in check in the system of government, the Governor-General has little effective power and must ultimately yield and accept the advice of the Prime Minister or Ministers.[36] The responsibility of the Governor-General to act on advice applies not only to constitutional functions but also arguably to ceremonial ones too.[37] The constitutional advisers to the Governor-General determine when Parliament sits, and when to hold an election in accordance with the rules of the Constitution. Thus, the Governor-General acts as a non-executive officer. His or her constitutional advisors, the Prime Minister and Ministers are the principle executive officers.

The executive authority: legal not political

Governing power rests with the Cabinet, which is a committee of the Prime Minister and key Ministers. 'Under the oversight of the Prime Minister, the Cabinet coordinates the activities of the Ministers.'[38] Each Minister heads a government department, and Ministers are accountable for their departments to the Parliament. All Ministers are bound by the collective decisions of Cabinet[39] – where legislative and government policy decisions are made. The significance of the Cabinet to our governmental functions is that: '[i]t is to Cabinet that the highest decisions of policy affecting Australia are brought. Often the questions arising involve intense conflict of interests or of opinion in the community. In Cabinet these conflicts have to be resolved. Decisions have to be taken in the public interest ...'[40]

'In the political, as distinct from the legal sense, then, the chief executive authority – and the authority chiefly responsible for legislative policy – is the Cabinet.'[41] Because of Cabinet's political function 'no legal powers or functions are conferred on Cabinet ... by the Constitution'.[42] In fact, the term 'Cabinet' is not an expression recognised in any formal constitutional documents.[43] Neither is the term 'Prime Minister'.[44] This is a legacy of our British inheritance, whereby almost all rules governing the Prime Minister and Cabinet are contained in constitutional conventions. Invariably, the executive's legal power is vested in other offices recognised in the Constitution, like the Governor-General, the Governor-General in Council or a Minister.

Frequently, a decision of Cabinet, which is to be implemented in law, requires a legal decision of the Governor-General or the Governor-General in Council.[45] The function of the Governor-General in this context is not political but legal. The Governor-General acting in council is not normally a deliberative forum, but decisions of Cabinet are noted there and thus become 'known to the law'.[46] The bulk of the Governor-General in Council's work is 'making proclamations, regulations and appointments to Government bodies and tribunals under ordinary legislation'.[47]

Australians see little of the Governor-General's formal legal role; they see more of the realpolitik of the Executive. The Prime Minister and Ministers are often pictured sitting around the Cabinet table. At other times the Chief Ministers, Prime Minister and Premiers are pictured at a conference, endeavouring to better allocate function and responsibility between the national and the State governments, or to address national problems.

Viewing the meetings of Cabinet, Prime Minister and Premiers, or seeing Ministers being questioned in Parliament, reinforces the role of elected officials exerting governmental power.

The reserve powers

Sometimes the Governor-General exercises real political powers which are vested in the office. These are the reserve powers, which constitute an exception to the rule that she must act on advice, and largely consist of powers to preside over elections or to choose who forms a government. Such powers include the discretion to dissolve the House of Representatives,[48] to call a double dissolution of both Houses of Parliament,[49] and to appoint and dismiss the Prime Minister and hence the government.[50] These are important 'meta-governmental' powers, which the Governor-General may exercise without, or contrary to, ministerial advice.

These residual powers are, on occasion, exercised through genuinely independent judgment. A Governor-General may be called upon to decide whom to invite to form a government, or whether to dissolve Parliament and allow an election or, on the other hand, invite another political leader to attempt to govern. Usually, the electorate determines the selection of the government. However, there are exceptional circumstances, such as when the Governor-General may take an active role in the formation of a minority government. This arises when a party who has obtained most, but not a majority, of seats in the popular House seeks to form a government. In this role, a Governor-General or a State Governor plays their part in providing for the smooth transition from one government to another. Such exercises of discretion are typically uncontentious, but there are times when the exercise of the reserve powers may be highly controversial because it can give rise to a constitutional crisis. And it is these constitutional crises that are headline news, propelling the Governor-General into the media spotlight.

Constitutional crisis

To understand the role of the Governor-General in exercising the reserve powers and how it can give rise to a crisis, it is necessary to look back at the tempestuous days in 1975. On 11 November (Remembrance Day), Sir John Kerr, the Governor-General, dismissed Labor Prime Minister Gough Whitlam. The origins of the crisis can be found in the powers and different compositions of the two Houses of the Federal Parliament. The Whitlam Government had a majority in the House, but not the Senate. Generally, the Senate possesses equal legislative power to the House of Representatives, including the power to defer or reject money Bills, but there is an exception: the Senate may not initiate or amend money Bills.[51] On 15 October 1975, the Senate deferred the government's supply (spending) Bills until the government agreed to a general election for the House of Representatives.[52] The disagreements between the Houses went back several years. 'The tactic of outright rejection was used frequently ...' during the government's term in office.[53]

As Liberal Senator Peter Durack remembered, '[this] was the most marvellous time to be in Opposition that anybody could ever possibly choose. We had more stimulating opportunities of resisting and attacking the government than any Opposition will ever have again'.[54] One independent senator, Reginald Turnbull, who generally supported the government, captured the feeling in the chamber some years earlier.[55] As far back as 1972, he prophetically said:

> What disturbs me is the smell of death in this chamber, of people waiting to kill. One can sort of smell this atmosphere of hate which is pervading this chamber and emanating from certain members on the Opposition benches. Of course they have the numbers. It is like the vultures ...[56]

As one Labor 'insider' aptly remarked of the Whitlam Government, 'Labor had never been in power. It had merely been in office'.[57] The government had remained steadfast for several years and the House of Representatives refused to accede to the latest demand. On 11 November 1975, Prime Minister Whitlam called on Governor-General Kerr to request the issuing of writs for a half-Senate election. Kerr immediately 'informed the Prime Minister that he had terminated the latter's commission' under section 64 of the Australian

Constitution.[58] He then appointed the Leader of the Opposition, Mr Fraser, as caretaker Prime Minister, on the condition that he secure passage of the supply Bills and advise him to call a general election of both Houses of Parliament. Mr Fraser agreed and won a landslide victory at the subsequent election.[59]

Protagonists view the resolution of the constitutional crisis of 1975 very differently. It might be regarded as a vindication of constitutional monarchy, the unhappy acceptance by Labor's leadership of the calling of an election, or the failure of responsible government. For constitutional monarchists, the resolution of the crisis is a vindication of Australian constitutional government. In Sir John Kerr's letter of dismissal, he believed his actions were the 'only solution consistent with the Constitution and with [the] oath of office and [his] responsibilities, authority and duty as Governor-General'.[60] Kerr found it necessary to find a 'democratic and constitutional solution'.[61] However, he did not discuss his solution with Mr Whitlam, fearing his own dismissal and involvement of the Queen.

Sir David Smith, Sir John's Secretary, recalls the manner in which the government was dismissed:

> The Whitlam government was removed from office as the Governor-General and the Prime Minister sat on opposite sides of the Governor-General's desk in the study at Government House, Canberra, and by Sir John Kerr handing Whitlam a letter ... A few moments later, the Fraser government came into office as the Governor-General and the Leader of

the Opposition stood on opposite sides of the Governor-General's desk, and by Fraser holding a Bible in his hand and taking the oath of office as Prime Minister ...[62]

For constitutional monarchist this was an orderly transfer of one government to another in a time of great political strain. Sir David Smith again explains:

> The politicians of those days put our Constitution under enormous strain, but it held firm; it did not crack. In what were admittedly somewhat unusual circumstances, what followed was a peaceful and orderly change of government, and we were immediately on the way to a democratic election that would enable the people to pass judgement on what had occurred. The events in Parliament and at Government House put our system of government to the most extreme test, but the system worked, and the processes of public administration did not miss a beat.[63]

To constitutional monarchists the dismissal was democratic because it referred the ultimate question to the people, and it was constitutional, for Sir John Kerr was exercising his reserve power under section 64 of the Constitution. The 1975 dismissal is also viewed very much as an act of public administration.

Supporters of Labor Prime Minister Gough Whitlam see the dismissal in a different way. To them, 1975 is regarded precisely as a constitutional crisis because an unelected official dismissed a democratically elected

Prime Minister. Sir John Kerr's actions might have been legal, but they were not legitimate. The Governor-General does possess the reserve power to dismiss a government, but his exercise in 1975 of that power was and has been challenged. For Gough Whitlam, the essence of the dismissal was secrecy:

> Secrecy was the absolute condition for the success of the intervention. But we are talking about secrecy sustained against the elected government and the Governor-General's constitutional adviser, the Prime Minister in unchallenged possession of the confidence of the House of Representatives.[64]

In Gough Whitlam's eyes, Sir John Kerr breached his constitutional duty. 'All Kerr had to do was his duty – his duty to be open, frank and honourable in his dealings with the Prime Minister. That way there could have been no ambush …'[65] Ultimately, the crisis was defused by the holding of the election. Labor's unhappy acceptance of the election was seen as a tribute to their leader's commitment to democracy. *The Australian* reflected upon the tumultuous events: '[t]here was no blood in the streets and no national strike. The response to the dismissal revealed the depth of Australia's commitment to democracy'.[66]

From another point of view, the precedent set by the 1975 crisis may be described as the low point of responsible government. Up until 1975, the Prime Minister and the government were responsible only to the lower House of Parliament.[67] After 1975, the political landscape was forever changed. Sir John Kerr justified his dismissal of Gough Whitlam, amongst other things, on the basis that the government was responsible for the passage of its spending Bills to both the House and the Senate.[68] He maintained that:

> Because of the principles of responsible government a Prime Minister who cannot obtain supply, including money for carrying on the ordinary services of government, must either advise a general election or resign. If he refuses to do this I have the authority and indeed the duty under the Constitution to withdraw his commission as Prime Minister.[69]

This view has been repudiated by Sir John's critics and defended by his supporters.[70] For instance, Gough Whitlam believed that the justifications Sir John Kerr offered, based on his understanding of responsible government, would ultimately undermine it. Another critic of Sir John's justification has remarked that it cannot be sustained on the orthodox principle of responsible government, since 'it is not possible for a government to be "responsible" to two Houses so elected that they can have different political majorities'.[71] Today, Sir John's actions and justification stand as a precedent. Nothing has changed constitutionally to prevent a recurrence, notwithstanding so much ink written on the pages of constitutional texts.[72] Time is ticking away, waiting for the next constitutional crisis.

The Constitution could be amended to remove

the power of the Senate to block supply, reaching the same position as the House of Lords in 1911.[73] Yet an amendment is unlikely because it would raise the divisive debates of 1975. Accordingly, most republican proposals leave these questions in abeyance. However, the power of the Senate to block money Bills arguably means that a future Governor-General may well have to take on a role in resolving a future constitutional crisis.[74] Time may heal the divisiveness of this debate and bipartisan support might exist for reform.

The 1975 crisis is not the only occurrence of a dismissal by a vice-regal officer. In 1935, the Premier of New South Wales, Jack Lang, was dismissed by the State Governor, Philip Game.[75] The grounds for dismissal were failure to comply with Commonwealth legislation, but this remained untested in the courts, giving rise to controversy.

Both the dismissal of the Lang Government and the Whitlam Government may be seen as premature. In the Lang dismissal '[t]he legal process was still available to test the legality' of the Premier's actions.[76] In the Whitlam dismissal, it was not clear that the government would have been unable to secure supply. It was solvent and had not been held to have breached any constitutional provisions.[77]

But what of the various view points of the 1975 constitutional crises? For constitutional monarchists the dismissals, premature or otherwise, stand as an endorsement of the effectiveness of Australia's system of public administration. For supporters of Prime Minister Whitlam, the resolution of the crisis depended upon his quality as an elected leader – but doubt must exist over reliance on leadership, for personality alone may either precipitate or inhibit resolution of further crises. For proponents of established principles of representative government, the 1975 crisis presents a dangerous and destabilising precedent. The two dismissals illustrate that crisis is part of Australian constitutional history. Yet these crises have been rare and Australian government has been stable.

Conclusion

It is vital to understand what the Governor-General does behind the scenes, and in public, in order to improve and enhance the role of a President in a future Australian republic. The 1975 crisis brought out into the public awareness the reserve powers of the Governor-General. The dismissal of the Prime Minister was greeted with disbelief by many, which is not a surprising response considering the brief media 'glimpses' the public has of the Governor-General. And the dispute was not so much about the legality, but the legitimacy of the Governor-General's actions.

Our glimpses of the Australian Constitution show that what it says is often not what happens in the practise of everyday government. This textual anomaly can be traced back to colonial and monarchical times.

Even in the Convention Debates to draft the Australian Constitution in 1897, delegate George Reid, the then Premier of New South Wales, proposed that the principle that the Governor-General acts upon advice of the ministry, be included in the Constitution,[78] a proposal rejected because it would be contrary to a drafting rule of the Imperial Parliament and monarchical convention.[79] Perhaps this result was the expression of the original cultural (constitutional) cringe! The political practice of government actors and most rules of parliamentary government are not often mentioned in the text of the Constitution, but have been left to constitutional conventions. This system only functions provided that all government actors accept the conventions and political practices. However, where there is a serious disagreement, there is a risk of a crisis. Sir John Kerr's position meant that he could be easily dismissed by the Prime Minister advising the Queen. And this precariousness influenced his decision to terminate the commission of the Prime Minister. Such a dismissal procedure did not apparently encourage him to adopt the democratic principles of transparency and openness.

We would do well, then, in drafting republican amendments to the constitution to say what it means in terms of political practice, as a way of offering certainty and clarity – and in keeping faith with some of the more far-sighted founders of the Australian Constitution. We should take the opportunity offered by republican reform to 'write the model of government we actually practice into constitutional law'.[80] Since our Constitution was drafted, many other countries have 'committed the rules of parliamentary government to constitutional law quite successfully'.[81]

This change would have the advantage of fostering constitutional literacy, a virtue in a democracy, and, most importantly, creating more effective restraints on the abuse of power by high political office holders.

5

The politics of minimalism

On 7 June 1995, Paul Keating gave his historic speech, *An Australian Republic: The Way Forward*. In this speech he provided a model which formed the basis of the proposal put to the people in the 1999 referendum. Most importantly, he introduced us to minimalism:

> The change we propose has very limited implications for the design of Australia's democracy. It is the so-called 'minimalist' option. All the essential Constitutional principles and practices ... will remain in place.[1]

Paul Keating then went on to explain the cultural significance of adopting a republican form of government:

> An Australian head of state can embody our modern aspirations – our cultural diversity, our evolving partnerships with Asia and the Pacific, our quest for reconciliation with Aboriginal Australians, our ambition to create a society in which women have equal opportunity, equal representation and equal rights. ... [W]e can give expression to both our best traditions and our current sensibilities and ambitions.[2]

Yet all of this was apparently based merely on the hope that an Australian as President would provide a symbol or, at most, an example of such aspirations. Almost anti-climatically, Paul Keating concluded that '[i]f only by a small degree an Australian republic fulfilled these ideals it would be worth it'.[3]

The minimalist argument was taken up by the Yes case in the 1999 referendum, when it was suggested that '[o]nly minor amendments to our Constitution will be required, and all of our democratic rights will stay the same'.[4] The Australian people were then asked to vote on a minimalist republic.

Minimalism rests on two interacting propositions: making the least possible constitutional amendments and doing so in a way that will induce important cultural change. These changes were intended to introduce a new national and cultural identity. Yet proposals for minimal constitutional change may represent a more momentous shift in democratic principles and political practice than is widely admitted.

Replacing the Queen as the head of state with a

President could have profound political consequences, not just cultural ones, since by changing our head of state we also change the political character of our government. Questions then arise: how might republicanism change Australia's political culture and institutions, and how might the adoption of an Australian head of state enhance democratic participation? Many of these questions were left unanswered in the republican debate. It was as if the proposal for an Australian head of state was put to the people without any resonance with a philosophy of republicanism. By republicanism I mean a philosophy of self-government which actively engages the citizenry.

There also remains another underlying question of whether altering the wording of the Constitution will introduce such political principles. Will a new constitutionalism be republican, or will it still contain the trappings of monarchism? Today some commentators regard Australia as a 'crowned republic', others argue that Australia is a constitutional monarchy and that only by purging the monarchy will Australia properly become a republic. Others have come to question the usefulness of minimalism!

Changing the Constitution, changing the political culture

The aim of the minimalist proposal is to remove the hereditary office of the monarch with only minor changes to the Australian system of government. Formal changes to the words of the Constitution would be required, such as replacing the term 'Governor-General' with the term 'President', while other changes would be consonant with the current understanding of how the constitutional and political system of government operates. Minimal proposals thus sever constitutional change from the broader idea of republicanism.

But is it so simple? After all, these amendments to the text of the Constitution itself are being made to invoke new political ideals and values. The first significant change will be to remove appointment and dismissal of the Governor-General by the Queen. This alteration will end the current relationship between the Queen and the Prime Minister, a connection which is relevant to the maintenance of the current Constitution and any proposed republican amendment which will replace the Queen with another sovereign figure: be it a President or the people. This is a change not often mentioned in the literature because the power vested in the Queen is perceived to be purely formal: to appoint and to remove the Governor-General.[5] Both functions are, by convention, performed only on the advice of the Australian Prime Minister. Nonetheless, this power is a constitutional restraint. The power of dismissal may never be exercised but its threatened use is a plausible check on an abuse of power by the vice-regal representative. Inversely, the possible threat of dismissal might precipitate a crisis. Indeed Sir John

Kerr, in the 1975 constitutional crisis, partly justified his actions in order to avoid involving the Queen in Australian politics.[6]

The Governor-General, as the Queen's representative, is tied to a monarchical tradition. Once the monarchical structure is removed the function of the monarch will certainly be lost and fade away.[7] This will, in turn, remove a restraint on the power of the head of state and the Prime Minister. In a time of crisis there would be no legitimating basis for political action by the head of state derived from the memory of the Crown, no historically based responsibility for guaranteeing the propriety of political power. Nor would there be any historically based constraint on the power of the head of state to intervene in the parliamentary domain, due to their role as the Queen's representative.

The second significant change will be to alter the foundation of authority of the head of state. The basis of our democracy will shift from a monarchical to a republican philosophy, and changing the mode of selection of the head of state changes the authority of the office holder. The simple phrases that: the Australian President 'is to be directly chosen by the people of the Commonwealth' and 'an Australian citizen be chosen as the President ... [as] affirmed by a two-thirds majority of the total number of the members of the Senate and the House of Representatives',[8] both introduce a different democratic basis of authority.

When the legitimating basis for the power of the

head of state changes to appointment by democratic and popular means, through an election of some form or other, the President then embodies the people's self-governing duties. A popularly elected President would get their authority through the legitimacy of a direct, popular and democratic assent, rather than gaining that authority from appointment by government. The justification for a President intervening in politics becomes a democratic one, and the basis of ultimate state authority changes too. In a republic the electorate retains ultimate and exclusive personal responsibility for determining which governors it is wise to select. Whereas in a monarchical tradition, even in the highly attenuated form found in Australia, ultimate personal responsibility for 'virtuous' government – government that is legitimate and conducive to political stability – rests with the monarch. Constitutional monarchy relies on the ideal of ultimate personal responsibility; that there is a single person – hopefully a person of wisdom and judgment – on whose shoulders governmental legitimacy rests.

Minimalists, though, might reply, contending that changing the mode of appointment will be confined only to what is provided for in the text and structure of the Constitution. No other express republican or democratic conferral of power is proposed to be included in the text of the Constitution itself. Accordingly, it will be a vital function of the constitutional text to limit or to constrain the use of governing power. However, providing for an election of the head of state will give rise to implications. This is because constitutions provide only brief principles for the operation of government.[9] The text and structure of the Constitution, as Professor Adrienne Stone has remarked, will often be 'too bare to provide clear guidance in any given case',[10] requiring reference to values or principles external to the Constitution.[11] The principle of representative democracy has already been recognised as an implication of the Australian Constitution.[12] It is not hard to envisage the election of the head of state giving rise to a democratic mandate.

Minimalists might contend, though, that one means to confine this mandate is to rely on constitutional conventions. These conventions have force as rules of political practice, they are a tradition which guides the Governor-General and the Prime Minister (such as that the Governor-General acts on the advice of the Prime Minister). It is contended that constitutional conventions will continue as conventions of Australian government, not monarchical government. While these conventions might act as restraints on a future Australian President, the basis of their authority will change. They will be founded on democratic and republican philosophy. The consequence of a new democratic and republican basis for authority is, of course, not a necessary result of a minimal alteration to the Australian Constitution, but in the choice of language we may invoke democratic and republican conceptions of the state.

The words and phrases of the Constitution, and political practice such as constitutional conventions, gain their meaning through our shared and, at times, contested understanding of values and philosophy. We might reasonably expect the Prime Minister and the President to act accordingly. Similarly, the behaviour of the Queen, Governor-General or, indeed, President will be informed by their own values, understandings and ethical systems.

In sum, as Justice Murphy of the High Court once remarked, 'Great rights are often expressed in simple phrases ...'.[13] Accordingly, changing the wording of the Constitution to introduce a republic will alter constitutional principles, practice and philosophy. But what then is a republican philosophy?

Constitutional monarchy or republican philosophy

The philosophy of constitutional monarchy can be contrasted with that of a republic as each differs markedly according to their political function, ruling and citizenship.

The political function of constitutional monarchy 'is to provide a non-elected figure' who is politically neutral, 'representing the unity and dignity of the state'.[14] The citizen is the subject (or beneficiary) of the Queen's peace, or army or court. Selection for political office is based on birth or patronage, god or tradition.

The political function of republicanism is not merely concerned with the replacement of the monarch with a popularly chosen President. Republicanism is more than the mere substitution of titles and, like the monarchy, it too has a history rich in meaning. This philosophy rests on the view that collective responsibility involves a commitment by the citizens to the ongoing political project of self-government.[15] Republicanism is concerned with establishing the conditions for political freedom in a nation state. These conditions necessarily include: an educated population committed to the well-being of the state; a habit of open political discourse; and the joining together of citizens, who are approximate political equals.[16]

Republicanism per se represents a different conception of leadership and ruling from that of a monarchy. It is, of course, profoundly anti-monarchical because it is about the rule by all citizens[17] and, accordingly, selection for political office should be open to all, and all should be engaged, in some way, in the conferral of office. Importantly, republicanism also expresses a different role for the citizen, where the citizen is a joint bearer of responsibility for the safety, sanity and efficiency of state power.

Republicanism thus presents a substantive version of popular government. It is important to recognise that republicanism is a philosophy that differs from the colonial notions of self-government. The republican vision was antithetical to the Imperial conception of colonial government because it fostered a dangerous and subversive philosophy of full independence.[18] Unlike colonial self-government, which ceded governing authority under the umbrella of the Empire, republicanism presents a vision of political independence, which proclaims the virtues of equality, deliberation, participation and citizenship.

Civic virtue and the idea of the common good are central to this conception of political life. The common good is a constitutive principle requiring that both citizens and political figures act in the public interest.[19] At its heart, republicanism has always been about the moral claims on citizens in political communities aspiring to self-determination. As Professor Cass Sunstein has observed:

> [T]he animating principle of [republicanism] was civic virtue. To the republicans, the prerequisite of sound government was the willingness of citizens to subordinate their private interests to the general good. Politics consisted of self-rule by the people; but it was not a scheme in which people impressed their private preferences on the government.[20]

This principle has been developed in early times, but its meaning has slowly evolved as it has been applied and reworked to the current day. Under classical republicanism, civic virtue was thought only possible in a direct democracy. An example of this is the town hall meeting, where people assemble to vote on community issues. It was thought that civic virtue could be the abiding concern and condition of local politics in small homogeneous communities, where there was a close connection between governmental action and the welfare of the community. However, at the time of American Independence, it was argued that large and diverse communities could also be created on republican lines. The shift in republican thinking was that civic virtue might be promoted in communities of millions of people through a system of political representation. According to James Madison, a republican political theorist and the fourth President of the United States, the engagement of citizens in government through a system of elected representation would, in fact, be superior because 'it may well happen that the public vote, pronounced by the representatives of the people, will be more consonant with the public good than if pronounced by the people themselves convened for the purpose'.[21]

However, the republican vision of politics has changed. Today, representatives rarely seem to act in aid of a common good. Consensus politics has declined because of the prevalence of factionalism, political conflict and political parties. These modern facts of life arise from that almost ubiquitous characteristic of civil society: 'The People' is a heterogeneous mixture with a diversity of identities, interests and political allegiances.[22] Conflict rather than consensus is a normal and even desirable part of our politics.[23] Representatives typically adhere to political allegiances, rather than acting in aid of the common good, and political parties dominate our parliaments. Nonetheless, in mature democracies, especially ones that mediate social diversity through a sophisticated system of political parties, traces of the republican conception of the common good can be found.

In Australian politics, there is a common interest in and general commitment to the continuity of the democratic process and democratic institutions. There are also common interests relating to certain substantive issues. For instance, a common opinion may be that public officers should be able to 'stand against the tide of corruption which is always ready to wash over the affairs of state'.[24] Likewise, in 1967, an overwhelming majority of Australians supported the constitutional recognition of the status of Aboriginal people.

A republican conception of politics still offers important insights and guidance for political actors. Republicanism confirms and enhances a general political vision which already exists in mature political societies including Australia. What is central to a revised republicanism, and to an attendant conception of its legitimacy, is that state power rests on the active engagement of citizens in the choice of governmental policies, in the conduct of government and in the selection of governors. Public discussion or the giving of reasons; the expression of needs, feelings and aspirations; and a willingness to talk and listen in order to reach an understanding, all determine the content of government.

In sum, the republican ideal is that 'voters should form and act on their judgments, and politicians form and act on their deliberations'.[25] But this view is not simply based on virtuous behaviour but rather prerequisites, which make civic virtue feasible. These prerequisites have now become part of our 'folk politics': 'the source of familiar ideas on limited tenure in public office, on the impeachability of officials, on the answerability of officials to forums of public debate and review, on the separation of executive and judicial authority, and on the bicameral division of legislative power'.[26] The promotion of civic virtue is therefore forged through a republican tradition based on law and opinion.

Republicanism is a particularly good philosophy for a future Australian President. But the way in which the new office of head of state is designed will be crucial. One function of the head of state – a commitment to the continuity of democratic institutions and politics – is a common rather than a particular interest. After all, the head of state is a single power-holder and should find a political base in deeper, more general notions of the political good. Moreover, self-interest may be harnessed to promote more general interests.[27] The President's interest in reputation may depend upon their forbearance from partisan politics, since this participation could destabilise and undermine the continuity of democratic government. Changing the arrangement for selecting the head of state to some form of general participation will also foster tendencies to seek out common political interests. Republicanism's deepest purposes go beyond anti-monarchism to a spirited opposition of privilege and of the promotion of narrow interests by government. As a result, republican notions of self-government may underpin the function of the head of state. The change to a republican head of state will also alter the notion of civic participation. Whether this occurs by direct election or approval by Parliament, Australians will be entitled to hold the office, and will have a say, whether directly or through representatives, in the choice of leader. This means notions of participation will be broadened and there will be a greater engagement of citizens in self-government. We might also expect greater civic pride in knowing that the head of state is an Australian. We might even expect that the stature of the office would grow, since the ceremonial function will be underpinned by Australian citizenship.

Distinguishing between monarchical and republican philosophy challenges the familiar notion that constitutional change will simply involve replacing the monarch with an Australian President. By considering these philosophies we deepen our understanding of the head of state debate. In this shift we may embrace the broader meaning of respublica and government for the common good.

Finding republicanism in Australia's past and future

The debate surrounding the republican initiative has caused both a revised understanding of Australian political philosophy and a renewed appreciation of certain constitutional principles. The republican revival has broadened the horizons of constitutional and political thought, and seen a flourishing of Australian historiography in the 1990s. As Professor Mark McKenna has remarked, republicans have located:

> republican principles in the word's etymology (that is, the Latin respublica – the public thing) or 'traditional' republican principles such as popular sovereignty, the rule of law, checks and balances, or the goal of a virtuous citizenry.[28]

Yet these principles have been obscured in Australian history. Republicanism was seen as a challenge to the formal institutions of constitutional monarchy.[29] To be a republican was to be disloyal, rebellious or even anti-Empire. Another reason for its invisibility is the perception of republicanism as a minority movement, a view challenged when the contemporary republican debate began in 1991.[30] Historians have shown the important contribution that republicans have made to Australia's political culture. Republican principles have also remained inconspicuous because political language is fluid. In *The Captive Republic*, Professor McKenna notes, '[a]lthough the word "republic" has remained the same, its meaning has not'.[31] Consequently, republicanism has proved elusive, and its long history is not typically that 'of a movement or even that of a consistently understood idea'.[32] Moreover, '"republican principles" in any period are likely to be contested'.[33]

Republican historians, such as Mark McKenna and Wayne Hudson, have responded by providing rich, diverse, multifaceted and contested histories of political, legal, social and cultural republicanism.[34] In particular, McKenna and Hudson's *Australian Republicanism: A Reader* enlivens our understanding by letting us hear the voices of so many republicans past.[35] Historians are making visible our past and contested history.

Republican proposals for constitutional change have given rise to a debate concerning the traditional principles of republican government, which might be remodelled for present-day politics.[36] With the re-emergence of the proposal for a republican head of state into the mainstream Australian political agenda, we might anticipate that there will be greater debate about the philosophy of self-government in a republic.[37] Greater agitation and argument for change may emerge again, embracing broader issues of constitutional reform such as the adoption of a constitutional bill of rights, enhancing participation by women in politics. Overall, the study of Australia's republican constitutional and legal principles, past and future, has moved well beyond minimalism.

The crowned republic

The plurality of the republican debate is illustrated by the use of the term 'crowned republic' to describe our system of government. The term was ushered in officially in 1993 by the Republic Advisory Committee established by Prime Minister Keating.[38] They justified their view by relying upon the ordinary meaning of a republic, as described in the *Macquarie Dictionary*, as a state in which:

- the supreme power rests in the body of citizens entitled to vote and is exercised by representatives chosen directly or indirectly by them
- the head of government is an elected president, not a hereditary monarch.[39]

They concluded that Australia is 'a state in which sovereignty resides in its people, and in which all public offices, except that at the very apex of the system, are filled by persons deriving authority directly or indirectly from the people'.[40] The Committee thought 'it may be appropriate to regard Australia as a "crowned republic" … in that the only Australian Office incompatible with a republic is the monarchy'.[41] The term 'crowned republic', it has recently been argued, is a more accurate description of Australian government today than constitutional monarchy. 'Britain has not been a Constitutional Monarchy since probably the late 18th century',[42] and today the phrase is 'massively out of date'.[43] Australia's system of government is better described as a representative democracy.[44]

Few would object to the claim that Australia is a parliamentary democracy and a nation state. However, the classification of Australia's system of government must depend upon context.[45] In the context of the head of state debate, it is more accurate in my view to describe Australia as a constitutional monarchy than a 'crowned republic'. This is because of the nature of our constitutional system.

Australia's legal and governmental systems are based on Australia as a monarchy,[46] with the Australian Constitution clearly expressing the monarchical character of Australian government.[47] The head of the federal and State governments is formally the Queen and her representatives. Not only is the Queen head of the executive but she is also an essential part of the Australian legislature and judiciary. As has been observed:

> The Queen or her representative is an integral part of each of the Australian parliaments: see, for example, Commonwealth Constitution s 1; *Constitution Act 1975* (Vic) s 15. Statutes of many state and the Commonwealth parliaments are described (in their opening words) as having been enacted by the Queen with the advice and consent of the houses of Parliament. Justice is administered by the law courts in the name of the Queen.[48]

Moreover, prosecutions by the state are carried out in the name of the Crown, with cases given such titles as *The Crown versus Smith*. The office of Queen is both hereditary and confined to persons of the Protestant religion in the *Act of Settlement 1701* (UK) s 1. And this Act does form part of the law received into Australia at the time of European settlement.[49] The Constitution vests considerable powers in the office of Queen. However, almost all of the executive powers are conferred by the Australian Constitution on the Governor-General of the Commonwealth as the Queen's representative.[50] While the Governor-General, not the Queen, exercises her powers and performs her duties, it would be wrong to see the role of the Crown as confined to the functions of Her Majesty as head of state or through her representatives. Indeed, the Commonwealth Government is also referred to as the Crown and it inherits many of its executive powers from the royal prerogatives. This is a particularly complicated area of substantive law and one that provides authority for the operation of executive power in Australia.

In addition, the monarchy is referred to throughout the Australian and State constitutions and operates through our legal institutions, the Parliament, the government and the courts. The reach of the monarchy extends beyond the legislation and the Constitution. The Queen's face appears on the five-dollar note and adorns all of our coins; many institutions and societies are named in her honour, such as the Royal Melbourne Hospital and the Royal Society for Prevention of Cruelty to Animals; and even pubs are furnished with monarchical titles like the Royal, the Prince Albert and the Prince of Wales. The vestiges of the monarchy permeate our cultural spaces as well as quietly playing a leading role in our social, political and legal systems.

Many of these symbols may go unrecognised or unnoticed because they have been and continue to be an important part of our social fabric. It is only when the Royal Women's Hospital rebrands itself as 'The Women's' that we have the opportunity to reflect upon their historical resonances. It is noteworthy that the Women's has kept its full royal title – albeit in lower case – but the emphasis has clearly changed. 'The Women's' is writ large on the side of the building. Even without a republican government, some of these symbols and titles are being replaced, or at least organisations are renouncing their monarchical origins. For example, barristers are now referred to as Senior Counsels rather than Queen's Counsels and the Royal Blind Society of New South Wales is now called Vision Australia.

It might have been thought that republican change would simply involve the important, though modest, task of 'switching formal symbols, sorting out the surrogate vice-regal heads of state, and rewriting the executive sections of the Commonwealth and State constitutions'.[51] But even proponents of this minimal view offer a cautionary note: 'changing formal language and switching symbols is relatively easy compared with issues of institutional design in devising an appropriate alternative structure for the office of head of state and combining this with parliamentary responsible government, if indeed that is to be retained in its traditional form'.[52]

Consequently, rewriting the Constitution is not so straightforward, as the Queen forms part of the judicial, parliamentary and executive systems. Removing the monarchical office requires consideration of the appropriate alternative structure for the office of head of state. This means that the choice between constitutional monarchy and republic cannot be explained simply in terms of the crowned republic. In fact, the description of Australia's system of government as a 'crowned republic' blurs the distinction between constitutional monarchy and republic, making the choice more complicated. There are important choices to be made in changing the workings, forms and symbols of our current and proposed systems of government. Even if the shift from monarchy to republic simply involved a change of forms and symbols, this would be a sufficient reason to justify the distinction between monarchy and republic. Indeed, the implications of the change raise important issues of public participation, the mandate of the President and notions of republican philosophy.

Conclusion

The republican philosophy challenges the minimalist conception of constitutional change which purports to maintain monarchical institutions and values. At referendum, the minimalist model did not convince the majority of voters.[53]

No longer then can it be asserted with confidence that a minimal change to the Constitution would simply leave current constitutional principles and practices intact. The central message of this chapter is that we cannot change our Constitution without also making changes to our political culture. In this, the absence of politics from minimalism has been called into question in four ways:

1 that a change to the wording of the Constitution will not change constitutional principles
2 that the philosophy of constitutional monarchy and republic may be distinguished
3 that the republican revival broadens our horizons beyond minimalist debate
4 that the concept of crowned republic obscures the choice between monarchy and republic.

Nonetheless, one aspect of minimalism is still widely accepted – retaining the current system of parliamentary government. Most recognise that a future Australian President should retain non-executive powers.[54] Only infrequently it is proposed that the new head of state be given substantial executive powers. However, as we have seen, the retention of our current parliamentary democracy may still require substantial change to our system of government.

We can leave the last word on minimalism to Paul

Keating, who recently commented that the virtue of his model 'was not its minimalism but its appropriateness to the Australian polity at the time when I proposed it'.[55] While the rhetoric of minimalism has faded, the central tenants of Keating's proposal – to maintain our current parliamentary system of democracy and a non-executive head of state – are of enduring importance. Rather than using the phrase 'minimalism', it would be better to argue for the continuance of our unique Australian form of democracy. In addition, we should argue for the adoption of a republican philosophy as the animating principle of our new presidential system. We should celebrate republicanism as a new form of government and a new way of engaging the citizenry; a vision that may in fact engage the voters too. Voters may be persuaded of the virtue of a head of state who guarantees the continuity of democratic government and acts in the common good of all. Ultimately either a direct or a parliamentary election for the head of state will enhance public participation in Australian democracy!

6

Between participation and neutrality: selecting the head of state

The republican debate is infused with values and ideals. Yet, these ideals often have to be compromised by practicalities to enable them to fit realistically into models of governance. Conflicts often arise over values, and addressing these is not easy. As Professor Martin Krygier has pointed out, few of us are used to arguing about matters of value in any sustained way:

> Our newspapers are full of facts and details, and often vehemently expressed opinions about them, but the values informing those opinions are rarely closely examined.[1]

So, values and ideals are often implicit. In Krygier's words, these are the beliefs left 'on the shelf', remaining as unexamined qualities frequently inherited from our parents.[2] The unexplored nature of our values or ideals leads to disagreements, and often these conflicts do not go away. Nor should we expect them to, since we weigh our values differently. But our values can be better understood by examining them and the disagreements that they give rise to.

Within the republican debate, people have disagreed most vehemently over the mode of appointment of the President. Those who argue for a parliamentary appointment are confronted by those who argue for a directly elected head of state. These differences ran so deep in the 1999 referendum that direct election republicans voted against the parliamentary election alongside constitutional monarchists.

Two important values underpinned this republican debate: neutrality and participation. It is interesting that these were some of the values that remained unexamined and were 'left on the shelf' in the popular debate. It is crucial then to commence a discussion about values and ideals by defining these terms, making them explicit and exposing them to the light of day.

Neutrality, in this sense, means that the head of state stays above the fray of politics. The head of state's role is to be non-partisan in a political dispute and tolerant of the political process. They should not publicly express a political preference, neither should they provide support for one side or the other – and no political party should be favoured.

Neutrality is regarded as a priceless value because it is vital to maintaining our current system of parliamentary democracy. Parliamentary democracy is seen as too precious and too important to risk in the hands of a head of state who will not act impartially. The ideal of a neutral head of state was forged from the hard-won compromise between the monarch and Parliament, meaning that real political power rests in the hands of our representatives. Our choice of representatives, not the choice of the head of state, determines government policy. Thus, those who advocate the value of neutrality see parliamentary democracy as a system worth defending.

For such republicans, the process of choosing the head of state ought to fit the neutral purpose of the office. The quintessential impartial head of state is the Queen of the United Kingdom presiding over a responsible parliamentary government (the Westminster system).[3] However, a parliamentary system of government under a republic is very different from one under a monarch. Unlike a monarchy, a republic is founded on democratic participation, a principle that should not be ignored in the crafting of the office of the new head of state.

Popular participation is of value because it is the sharing of power between the people, the Parliament and the head of state. Initially, the people must vote to choose a model for a republic, and subsequently the people or their representatives must periodically choose the office holder. Participation possesses the virtues of inclusion and diversity, and in a democracy participation requires popular choice. This value may be given expression in two ways: direct election or parliamentary selection of the head of state. We might take popular choice for granted because we regularly vote in elections, but it must not be forgotten that the struggle for the franchise was hard fought. The ballot box has provided us with engagement with the political process, accountability and political stability. Of course, there are very different notions of popular choice.

Advocates of a direct election of a President see the vote as the highest form of popular involvement, imparting the greatest trust in elected officials, and hence the most democratic system. For them, direct election is worth striving for as an extension of the right to vote. Advocates of a direct election might make their point this way: under the current system the Prime Minister and Cabinet choose the Governor-General, which means twenty people acting behind closed doors make the decision.[4] Under the 1999 referendum model, a two-thirds majority of Parliament would choose the head of state. This means that 225 people would be making the decision.[5] In addition, a presidential nomination committee, comprised of 32 Commonwealth, State, Territory and community representatives, was to be established to receive public nominations and make recommendations to the Prime Minister. Under direct election proposals the voters would choose the President, meaning that if the vote was to be held in 2009 13 801 216 people would make the decision.[6]

Direct election is the clear winner. It is the most democratic method with more people making the decision than under any other proposal. Direct election is certainly appealing but is it an irresistible argument?

Advocates of parliamentary election see things very differently. Yes, voting is important and vital, but popular choice is not just a numbers game; it involves both the leaders and the people. Under a parliamentary democracy, the elected representatives are entrusted with governmental decisions since parliamentarians have the inclination, time and resources to hopefully make a wise decision.

Most importantly, unlike voting, where individuals make the decision on their own, representatives make their decisions collectively. Each decision-making process is very different. When we vote, we may discuss our views with others but we each vote individually at the ballot box. By contrast, representatives decide by agreeing to, or accepting, the views of others in their party room or in the Parliament. Representatives also jointly evaluate criteria for high office, such as merit, commitment and popular support. There is a discipline to collective choice because compromise may motivate the decision and joint scrutiny may increase the stakes, rigour and intensity of the process.

Having defined our values, we now consider two key questions about selection of the head of state:

1. How do different modes of selection provide for a politically neutral head of state?
2. How do different modes of selection involve popular control by the people and their representatives?

The value of this inquiry is to be found in the explanation of the values of participation and neutrality. But further questions do arise. How do the different methods bear upon the choice between the philosophy of monarchy and republic considered earlier? Should neutrality trump participation? Can any apparent conflict be resolved by providing effective means of popular control over selection of the head of state?

Executive appointment: the current method

Currently the Queen appoints and dismisses the Governor-General on the advice of the Australian Prime Minister.[7] Her decision is purely formal; according to constitutional convention she has no choice but to accept a Prime Minster's candidate. The real decision rests elsewhere – with the Cabinet, which only meets behind closed doors, ensuring the confidential vetting of candidates.

Popular control is maintained through the principle of responsible government, founded on the history of the British monarchy. Under that convention, the choice is vested in the Prime Minister and Cabinet. Because the Cabinet are also members of Parliament, their decision represents the choice of the electors delegated to the government they chose. The constitution vests the government with such a choice, and we trust their judgment for other executive decisions such as the appointment of High Court judges.[8] Government members of Parliament would also be informed or consulted about the prospective candidate. The current system is designed to produce a candidate who will refrain from participating in partisan politics. This is partly achieved through the selection process itself where:

- candidates are not likely to be chosen if they would actively oppose or undermine the government
- candidates' ideological leanings and backgrounds must be acceptable to the government
- office holders are expected to act neutrally
- safe and trustworthy candidates are the norm.

It is highly unlikely that a candidate selection would be questioned by the Parliament. Mostly, this is because the choice is constitutionally vested in the government not the Parliament. The democratic norm is that the opposition will accept the constitutional right of the government to make certain decisions because the government has a mandate from the people. It is also likely to be counter-productive to challenge the appointment of a Governor-General who may, in fact, be serving in office when the opposition comes into government! Overall, the decision is made by the government, not the Parliament or the people.

Parliamentary appointment: the 1999 referendum model

The referendum proposal might simply be seen as the Parliament replacing the Queen, and therefore the Cabinet, as the appointing authority of the head of state, but this neat distinction is not grounded in realpolitik. We have to look beyond symbols to the procedures and practices of appointment, which is where the realpolitik lies. The 1999 Constitutional Convention proposed a nominations committee as well as selection through Parliament.[9] The steps were:

1. Nominations are provided to the Prime Minister by the Presidential Nominations Committee.
2. In the House of Representatives the Prime Minister moves and the Leader of the Opposition seconds a motion that a named Australian citizen be chosen as the President.
3. The motion is affirmed by a two-thirds majority of the total number of the members of the Senate and the House of Representatives.

The purpose of the two-thirds majority vote in

Parliament was to select a candidate who has bipartisan support. Hence the name: the bipartisan model. Moreover, this form of selection process would be in accordance with traditional republican principles. In the words of America's fourth president, James Madison, representation would:

> refine and enlarge the public views by passing them through the medium of a chosen body of citizens, whose wisdom may best discern the true interest of their country, and whose patriotism and love of justice, will be least likely to sacrifice it to temporary or partial considerations.[10]

Under the two-thirds majority model, party and factional considerations would be minimised. Partisan politics may not be entirely removed though, since the candidate would be nominated by the government. But because only a candidate acceptable to both the government and the opposition would be chosen, the appointment should be elevated above party politics. A candidate able to obtain the 'affection' of conflicting parties would also be a visible symbol of unity.[11]

The selection process invokes other republican principles: the check and balance. Proposal of a candidate by government after considering the views of the Nomination Committee would offer a considered and balanced decision-making process. The check would be provided by the opposition, which is granted a veto. It would probably become customary for the Opposition not to frustrate the process, since centrist candidates would likely be nominated.

Turning from the function of the bipartisan model in producing a politically neutral head of state, it is important to consider its other function: to enhance popular control of candidate selection. Parliamentary selection is founded upon the classic conception of representative democracy, where the people directly choose their representatives who, in turn, choose the head of state. However, the process does not adhere to the pure theory of representative democracy. Formally all members of Parliament are entitled to a vote, but substantively the ballot is governed by party allegiance. Further departures from the pure theory of representative democracy are that only one candidate will be nominated and the vote is not a simple majority. Nonetheless, this is still an effective choice based on the two-party system. The candidate will need to be supported by a two-thirds majority, necessitating the support of the government and opposition, but not necessarily the minor parties or independents. Nonetheless, a greater majority which might include minor parties may frustrate the process entirely. Overall, the bipartisan model reflects the status quo of two-party politics, yet the realm of the political is broader and more diverse.

It was therefore proposed to broaden the basis of the President's authority. It was envisaged that the President could be appointed based upon what might be described as a principle of fair reflection. That is, the head of state over time would come to represent people from a diverse range of backgrounds and experiences. The means to achieve this objective was through the Nominations Committee. The Prime Minister would consider the Report of the Committee in proposing the nomination to Parliament.[12] The Committee would also be a consultative mechanism which would enable popular input into the decision.[13] The purpose of this process was to enhance selection of suitable candidates who would command the respect and support of the Australian community.[14]

Many thought that it would be symbolically important to have more women or Aboriginal people, and people of different cultural backgrounds, holding the office. Such people might act as role models. The office of the President was to play a significant part in the formation of a new national identity. However, some more radical critiques have suggested that the inclusion of an Aboriginal figure or a woman might reinforce exclusionary practices.[15] For instance, an Aboriginal person as a head of state might dampen Aboriginal enthusiasm for Aboriginal sovereign self-government.[16] It is likely that any person chosen 'would be safe, solid and conservative, unlikely to rock any boats'.[17] More radical figures, likely to raise issues from their own backgrounds and experience, would be unlikely to be chosen. The good behaviour of most Governors or Governors-General has meant that they have been relatively invisible to the public eye.[18] However, the symbolic significance of a woman as Governor-General, such as Quentin Bryce, ought not to be underestimated. Bryce has already changed the perceptions of the office. For example, she has withdrawn the Governor-General's patronage of the Australian Rifle Association.[19]

The 1999 referendum model was criticised too as the politician's republic. This was because the head of state was to be chosen by parliamentary representatives – not the people. In response to this criticism it is argued that under a system of representative democracy it is the right and the duty of the representatives to make executive appointments. Moreover, the Constitutional Convention model was designed to produce a bipartisan figure who was not a politician. To the electorate, the two-thirds majority procedure may add little to the current scheme of two-party democracy. In other words, it does not improve upon it. But democracy is more than the two-party system and votes in Parliament. It embraces diversity. The nomination process was designed to achieve a fair reflection in the backgrounds, identities and experience of the office holder. But this was not enough for some, who wanted the so called 'people's republic'.

Direct election: the non-executive President

Popular election raises important questions. Can a popularly elected President act as a politically neutral figure compatible with our current parliamentary system of government? Will popular election really differ from choice by the Parliament? Many who favoured direct election, criticising parliamentary appointment as the politician's republic, were met with the somewhat ironic response that in fact there was no better way than a direct election to ensure the selection of a politician as President!

There have been two criticisms of direct election. First, that popular choice is likely to result in a politician for President. Candidates are likely to be members of political parties, mega-stars, extremely wealthy individuals or backed by wealthy interests,[20] as these are the only people likely to have the funds to run a national election campaign. Those who have previous political experience will be well suited to run for office. Advocates of direct election do not see this, necessarily, as a problem. As Professor Winterton noted:

> This may well be so, but it would be wrong to assume that a former politician could not serve as competently and impartially in the presidency as former politicians have as Governor-General ... Moreover experience in other direct-election parliamentary republics, such as Ireland, Austria, Iceland and Portugal, suggests that former politicians are quite capable of shedding their former partisanship and becoming impartial Heads of State.[21]

The second criticism of direct election is that an unsuitable person would be chosen for the office. Certainly, an elected President would be a very different kind of person to one who might accept a parliamentary appointment. It is thought that 'direct presidential election would detract from the necessary excellence and impartiality of the Head of State in our governmental system'.[22] What is meant by this argument is that such a person might be unsuitable, radical or even a populist candidate! Would Dame Edna Everage, the much-loved but fictitious cultural icon be elected? Frankly, Barry Humphries may make for a very interesting President. By contrast, parliamentary appointments are likely to be people with specialist expertise in law and politics, which may not be gained through work in the public eye. While it would be beneficial to widen the pool of candidates to those who might not ordinarily run for a political office, it is hard not to see the criticism of popular candidates as patronising and undemocratic.

While popular politics is at times vulgar and uncomfortable, to allay fears or concerns, direct election supporters argue that unsuitability has not proved to be a problem in other direct election republics, such as Ireland, Austria and Portugal.[23] As one commentator has said:

> About half the parliamentary republics in the world have popularly elected presidents and half do not, and it does not seem to make a dime's worth of difference, because every elected president operates within a framework of clearly understood, and very limited powers.[24]

Yet another concern is that a popular election might give rise to a different kind of unsuitability, a type with more sinister motives – an autocrat rather than merely a demagogue. Since Athenian times democrats have been concerned with 'autocratic politics', and since the American Revolution with political parties or factions who act contrary to the citizenship rights of others and the common good of the polity.[25]

Political thinkers have responded by devising a variety of checks on selection to prevent abuses of power, regulating participation to ensure the continuity of the 'necessary and ordinary operations of government'.[26]

Ultimately, the selection of the best candidate will rely upon the good judgment and common sense of the Australian people.[27] However, advocates of a politically neutral head of state have argued that Australians must be given the choice of candidates with acumen, skill and engagement. They have sought to adapt the processes of direct election to produce candidates who will act neutrally and be of an outstanding calibre. The processes of popular election are well known. The candidate must be qualified, nominated and elected. Important democratic principles underpin each of these different democratic processes. But will the measures to promote neutrality instead result in a diminution of the freedom of electors to choose their representatives? Will such limitations unjustifiably rule out suitable candidates?

Qualifications

The qualifications for office provide the eligibility criteria. In a democracy the eligible are those who are capable of being chosen – those who can vote can run for office. There are two critical criteria: a candidate must be an Australian citizen and eighteen years of age.[28] Citizenship is the obvious qualification for an Australian President, in contrast to the current hereditary office of the monarch. In a democracy, the people rule because 'popular control means that all adults share in political power'.[29] The universal franchise is the guiding principle: all those capable of choosing are entitled to vote and all those capable of being chosen are entitled to stand for Parliament.

In Australia, though, some people are disqualified from participating in elections.[30] The grounds of exclusion generally relate to those who are not regarded as fit or proper – the unfit are those incapable of choosing and the improper those who do not conform to social convention or are not appropriate. Some of these disqualifications seem obvious; a prisoner ought not to be able to sit in Parliament. But such justifications cannot necessarily be sustained in accordance with the principle of universal suffrage since even a prisoner is capable of being chosen, although not sitting in Parliament.[31] Such a restriction might also exclude the choosing of candidates like Nelson Mandela. According to the principle of universal suffrage everyone is assumed to be capable of choosing. Fitness has nothing to do with capacity; even incapacity does not prevent the capability of choice. Thus, as Professor Mayo concludes: 'There is no logical stopping place short of universal adult suffrage.'[32] Only reasons external to the rationale of the universal franchise may justify the exclusion.

For a long time now, '[t]here is little serious questioning that the franchise should be co-extensive with all adults ... The differences of sex, race, religion or wealth' have been regarded as irrelevant for many decades in Australia – to the extent that the suffrage is less than universal, there is less popular control and less democracy.[33]

Nomination

Nomination is the official process by which a candidate is proposed for election. It is one thing to nominate one's self, and another to be nominated by the government for the office. At least three options for nomination have been suggested:

1 Nomination for all
2 Restricted nomination
3 Nomination by Federal Parliament or a nomination committee.

These options are not mutually exclusive. Instead, nominations might be made through various processes or even a set of stages.[34]

Nomination for all

The freedom to run for office is the guiding democratic principle here, which entitles all those capable of standing to nominate for office. This freedom is necessary if there is to be a meaningful choice by the people at the polls, which in turn depends upon whether people are free to present themselves at an election. The freedom is principally for the electors rather than the candidates, by providing a live choice at the polls. No freedom is absolute; and some minor limitations may be justified. The freedom is not regarded as violated by minor restrictions such as a requirement to obtain 'a few signatures of friends on the nomination paper' or 'a deposit fee'.[35]

While this principle applies to parliamentarians, should it apply in the same way to a President? After all, the President is elected from the whole country whereas parliamentarians are elected from a locality or a State. The vast size of the electorate might necessitate some further restrictions.

Restricted nomination

A restricted model of nomination proposes several limits including:

- Citizens may nominate if they pay a deposit fee.
- Citizens may nominate provided they can demonstrate popular support.

Nominations for the Federal Parliament currently require a deposit fee: $500 for the House and $1000 for the Senate. The payment is refundable for successful candidates and secured for the privilege of running for office.[36] Of course, money acts as an obstacle to the frivolous, though not the wealthy! The cost perhaps avoids a ballot paper the size of a tablecloth and it forces candidates to demonstrate a level of seriousness by providing a financial commitment. But such a fee ought not to be so great as to deny the public the choice of a serious candidate.

The other limitation is that citizens may nominate provided they can demonstrate popular support.[37] The rationale of the limit is that the number be 'large enough to ensure that only candidates with a realistic prospect of election are nominated, but not so large as to be prohibitive'.[38] One proposal would require that a presidential candidate must obtain the signatures of about 1 per cent of the electorate (138 121), which is much larger than a country like Portugal's requirement of 0.75 per cent, but about the same as Iceland.[39] Requiring the candidate to obtain over 130 000 signatures would definitely demonstrate sufficient popular support to be realistically elected. In addition, nomination by a substantial population is more likely to spot an unsuitable candidate, such as one with autocratic tendencies.

However, obtaining such a large figure may be prohibitive for most individuals. It is only the wealthy, celebrities, and members of political parties or other large groups who could gain such support. Such a large number may be seen as discriminatory by powerful groups against outsiders.[40] At the other end of the spectrum, a nomination form might require perhaps 50 or 500 signatures, which is likely to be more realistic for active citizens or perhaps even small political parties, and provide a measure of popular viability. Fifty is the number currently required for nomination for the Federal Parliament and 500 is the number required for recognition of a political party.[41] The critical mass of such numbers might provide a base from which the citizen might draw to run an election campaign.

Even so, given the Australian experience of branch stacking, 50 signatures seems too few and even 500 may not be a viable filter against corruption. Thus, choosing the requisite numbers of signatures for nomination may require a fine balance between avoiding corruption, demonstrating popular support and not unduly restricting the freedom to run for office.

Nomination by the Federal Parliament or a nomination committee

Nomination by the Federal Parliament alone of at least three candidates,[42] would certainly address problems of the frivolous candidate and perhaps the need for a deposit fee. The process of selecting the person through Parliament might be conducive to scrutiny and care in selection of appropriate candidates too.

The President's mandate may also be restricted because it derives legitimacy not just from the people but also from Parliament. An exclusive parliamentary nomination system exists in Ireland, where twenty or more members of Parliament from at least four counties nominate presidential candidates who are directly elected by the people. One rationale for parliamentary nomination was to exclude small, extremist groups gaining attention for themselves by unrealistically running their candidate in an election. This occurred in Germany: 'in 1932, when Nazi leader Adolf Hitler had run against the incumbent President, Paul vön Hindenburg. Hitler had no chance of winning, but the election gave him a convenient platform on which to attract national attention'.[43]

Critics of exclusive nomination regard it as an appeal to the 'politics of illusion'.[44] While in theory the people democratically elect their President, they choose from a narrow list of candidates.[45] Some believe that dissenting views are best expressed within the political system rather than excluded from it. It ought not be forgotten that the requirement that candidates present themselves for an election will involve a competitive, open and strenuous process of scrutiny and can, in fact, provide checks and balances of suitability.

Parliamentary nomination alone may cause any new system of government to be seen as the politicians' republic, as the three candidates may reflect the three dominant parties.[46] The parliamentary nomination of a greater number of candidates may diminish this criticism. Even so, restricted nomination via Parliament arguably violates the fundamental freedom to run for office, and by restricting the choice, electors are denied a lively mix of candidates at the polls. The choice of nomination should rest with the people, not only the Parliament, in a directly elected model.

The virtues of nomination as a means of exclusion must be questioned, but nomination as a means of inclusion is justifiable. Parliamentary nomination may enhance the pool of suitable candidates. In any democratic process it is useful to have ways to find and nominate suitable candidates, and roping in candidates who would not otherwise offer themselves for election, will enhance choice. Potential exclusions perceived prior to the 1999 referendum included criticisms that women and people from regional areas might be disadvantaged in running for office.[47] Thus, citizens could be nominated by a specified number of members of the federal or State parliaments as an additional means of nomination rather than an exclusive one. This might be a way to overcome potential problems of geographical exclusion of some candidates, or the hurdles posed to disadvantaged groups. In addition, a nomination committee, along the lines proposed in the 1999 referendum model, could act to nominate candidates. As mentioned earlier, the virtue of the committee is that it would select meritorious candidates from diverse backgrounds. The challenge today may be to find people outside the political realm who have the necessary skills, experiences and abilities to enhance our democracy.

Both parliamentary and committee nomination provides a way to broaden the pool of candidates who might not obtain the necessary popular support but might be highly suitable: distinguished, diverse and capable. Nonetheless, any such nomination procedures will act as a filter by providing for elite selection and privileged nomination by political representatives. There may be a perception, though, that any nomination process that ropes in candidates will give them unfair advantage. Lying at the heart of the freedom to run for office is that all should have the same opportunities. Do popular support and viability then provide the only justifiable limitation? There is an important difference between a group of members of Parliament nominating an initially reluctant local candidate, and selection of candidates by Parliament as the only choice. Members of the community may gain satisfaction nominating the unlikely but the suitable, increasing the pool of candidature. The adherence to democratic principles depends upon the interaction between these processes: are they mutual and interlocking or are they exclusive? There is no practical reason why there should be one mechanism alone.

Voting

Popular election has all the attractions of direct democracy. The voters directly choose the candidate, unlike in a representative system where the representatives directly choose the office bearer. Representative government is therefore an indirect form of democracy. In a direct democracy the control over the decision rests with the people themselves.[48] And it is the people who will have the last word.

The vote is premised upon political equality, the equality of all adult citizens in voting. The attraction of this principle is found in the traditional catch cries of democracy: one person, one vote, and each vote counts equally.[49] In an electoral system based on equality of voting, it is assumed that the candidate will be selected by a majority of the voters, and hence it is that the majority rule. However, different electoral systems may alter this principle. In a first-past-the-post system, where the candidate with the most votes wins, a person who obtains less than the majority of votes may still be chosen.[50] Hence, it is likely that the Australian system of preferential voting will be preferred, since the candidate who is preferred by 'an absolute majority (more than 50 per cent) of the formal vote', is the one chosen.[51] The two-stage process – where there is a second ballot between the two leading candidates if no candidate obtains more than 50 per cent of the votes in the first ballot – that occurs in some countries may not be chosen because of both expense and expediency.[52]

It is easy to see the attractions of direct election. You get to choose the candidate, your vote counts the same as everybody else's, and the candidate preferred by the majority wins.

All citizens may get to have their say, but what does this communicate to the incoming President? Such an office holder would have a popular mandate from the people enabling them to act more independently. The head of state would have a new voice, the voice of the elected leader of the people. There would be a reconfiguration of the state, which would require a reconfiguration of the political order. The head of state, as a single power holder, might have a greater authority than a Prime Minister, whose mandate is indirectly conferred through Parliament and support for the goals of his/her party. For proponents of the current system, there is a concern that formally or informally the head of state will gain a political independence permitting them to act well beyond the current sphere of the Governor-General.[53] There are three possible expansions in the powers of the current Governor-General: voice, policy formation and an active checking role.

The head of state's voice might be transformed through both a parliamentary and popular election. To appreciate the change in voice it is necessary to compare the current Governor-General's role with that of a parliamentary and popularly elected President. While the main 'technique of power exercisable by the Governor-General is the public expression of personal opinions', the 'selection process seems designed to ensure that her opinions would not be "controversial"'.[54] However, the parliamentary mandate will give a President greater authority than a Governor-General. The opinions of both a parliamentary elected and a popularly elected President would be more widely reported and noted. Moreover, a directly elected President may come to see the platform on which they ran – the public awareness of their opinions – as legitimating their voice because they were endorsed by the public.

A popularly elected presidency might become a new state institution separate from the elected government[55] and the process of election itself might give rise to policy proposals, arguments and debate. The President might make funding commitments and formulate policy. They could be lobbied for political ends of politics.[56] Questions may arise as to how the President might hear and respond to political claims.[57]

Supporters of presidential neutrality seek to restrict the capacity of the head of state to develop a new bureaucratic apparatus with the capacity for formulation of policy. While they admit it would not be possible to limit what is said in election campaigns, support for the development of independent governing power could be constrained.[58] Without such limits, the current government policy formulation might be frustrated and undermined. Under our current system, the Prime Minister and Ministers research and develop policy with the advice of government departments and they may be questioned in Parliament. Our current system also provides an opportunity for participation, for input by citizens in developing government policy, through contact with government Ministers, government departments and local members.

Yet another proposed role for a directly elected President is to take on an active checking role of the Prime Minister and government, providing opposing centres of authority.[59] There have been criticisms, though, of such an independent role for the President. First, the President would be unaccountable, certainly to Parliament and perhaps to the electorate, if they are a single-term holder and their mandate is out-of-date.[60] Secondly, such a new role, which would be at variance with the current function of the Governor-General, might lead to deadlock and instability in our political system.[61] Thus, a popular election raises implications about the powers and functions of a head of state.

In this chapter it has been assumed that the head of state would maintain their current powers. Even so, the ways in which a parliamentary and popular election may change those powers and functions will be considered in chapter 7. Popular election, though, remains justifiable for a non-executive President, one which does not possess powers to formulate policy or to actively check a Prime Minister. Since, why should the people not have a say in choosing the highest political office holder in the land? The President's status and power would grow with popular election giving them a new voice, which may enliven democracy.

Overall, there is a logic to popular election. All adult citizens are eligible and ought be able to nominate for the office where the people have the final say. Serious candidates and well-qualified candidates ought to be encouraged. However, as I have noted above, this system cannot be introduced without considering some of the problems that are intrinsic to its operation.

Popular sovereignty

The republican philosophy of popular sovereignty is also invoked by proposals to reform our head of state,[62] which is seen as the natural source of legitimacy to replace the monarchy.[63] The direct election of the President adheres most closely to notions of popular sovereignty, which is the belief that popular authority is derived from the vote of the people[64] – one person, one vote[65] – unlike the referendum model where the authority was derived from their representatives.[66]

The theory of popular sovereignty also has implications for the Constitution. Nowhere is the term popular sovereignty explicitly mentioned. In fact, the Constitution itself is an Imperial Act of the UK Parliament. The traditional view, then, is that the authority of the Australian Constitution is found upon an Act of British sovereignty.[67] However, some scholars argue that indeed the Australian Constitution is founded upon the principle of popular sovereignty, since it provides for popular elections.[68] Moreover, amendment of the Constitution is provided for through a popular vote in a referendum. So the argument runs, the people who have not voted for change in a referendum have acquiesced in the continued operation of the Constitution.[69] The language in the preamble, which was once thought to invoke British sovereignty, has now been reclaimed to invoke popular sovereignty. That the 'people agree to unite in one indissolvable federation ...' is seen as appealing to popular sovereignty, but in fact it must be remembered that the agreement mentioned in the preamble was made 'under the Crown' and by the 'people of the [read British] colonies'.[70]

It appears that Australia is both a constitutional monarchy and a state resting on popular sovereignty. To resolve the potential contradictions republicans can offer two reforms:

- Patriation of the Constitution, meaning to bring it home. This means that the Australian Constitution should be enacted as an Australian Act of Parliament, not a British one. As a result of this proposal, the Constitution would recognise explicitly that sovereignty lies in Australia, not in the United Kingdom.
- Sovereignising the people, by an express mentioning of popular sovereignty in the Australian Constitution. The Constitution would acknowledge that the authority of government derives solely from

its people, that the people have sovereign power, which they then vest in government.

'Patriation' and 'Sovereignsing the people' are not words necessarily found in any dictionaries, but we as Australians can give them our own meaning. With both reforms we can draw inspiration from experience overseas. The Canadians were the first to patriate their Constitution in the early 1980s. Many countries acknowledge that their constitutions rest on the will of the people. In the United States Constitution the preamble reads: 'We the people of the United States ... do ordain and establish this Constitution for the United States of America.'[71] The preamble of the Constitution of India reads: 'We, the people of India, having solemnly resolved to constitute into a sovereign socialist secular democratic republic ...'[72]

Constitutional scholars, such as Professor Saunders, have urged the view that the Constitution should state that the will of the people is the authority for the Constitution. Such a reform could be consistent with a parliamentary or a popular head of state.

Conclusion

Participation and neutrality confront each other in the republican debate. By exposing these values, we confront their differences in the modes of selection: executive appointment, parliamentary appointment and popular election. Republicans, though, have been caught between participation and neutrality.[73] How then can we respond to this conflict?

The pursuit of neutrality can be seen as stifling the chances of gaining participation. Advocates of neutrality who have favoured parliamentary appointment see it as the best means to create a head of state above partisan politics. Yet their efforts to foster participation through establishing a nomination committee to broaden the range and diversity of candidates have been seen as limited. Advocates of neutrality who have favoured a direct election argue that it is necessary to control the nomination process, restricting candidates. But these limits threaten to undermine the freedom of electors to run for office, qualifying complete democratic participation.

Advocates of direct election who have become preoccupied with participation are at the risk of ignoring the value of neutrality. They argue that the Australian people should have the right to vote for their President. But it must be acknowledged that an election gives a mandate, a possibly dangerous and destabilising power.

The catch can be undone in each mode of selection by more fully explaining and justifying the subordinate value. Advocates of direct election have the burden of showing how they would create a staunchly neutral head of state. Advocates of parliamentary election have the burden of showing how the system is sufficiently participatory.

Between neutrality and participation, other values have informed the debate. Perceptions of limitations are important. Restrictions that would unduly fetter values of participation may in fact undermine it. A popular mandate without limitations may in fact destabilise democracy. There is a fine balance between neutrality and participation in each model.

Some parliamentarians are prejudiced against popular mandate, because they know its power. Some popular electionists are prejudiced against politicians, believing they will select someone from an elite group. Prejudice is addressed by exposing it, and in a democracy openness and criticism are strengths.

Power is also an important value in the sense of who has control over the decision. Power in this context is seen as a thing, something to be held or possessed. Direct electionists want the power to rest in the hands of the people. Advocates of the parliamentary election want to vest it in parliamentarians, indirectly vested in the electors. But power can be understood as empowerment through a foundational narrative. Under our current system, the Queen is our head of state and the Governor-General is her representative. In a republic, ultimate power rests with the will of the people. So popular sovereignty will replace British sovereignty. Patriation provides a unifying metaphor to reinvigorate our notions of national identity and sovereignty.

In this chapter, we have examined how to enhance popular participation in the selection of a new office of head of state, and its implication for maintenance of our system of a politically neutral head of state. It is now important to consider how to establish a new office of President in a way that maintains a politically stable system of government. To achieve this we broaden our study beyond neutrality and participation to consider issues of legitimacy and legality.

7

(Mis)behaviour in republican Australia

We live in an age of crisis. The headlines tell the story: the Global Financial Crisis, 9/11 and global warming are but a few of the 'emergencies' that now dominate global discourse.[1] Even before 9/11, the philosopher Giorgio Agamben argued that the language of crisis had become the normal discourse of our politics.[2] Before the planes crashed into the Twin Towers of the World Trade Center in New York City on 11 September 2001, the republic debate stirred fears of crisis and misbehaviour. The question for us then and still today is: Does republicanism present an uncertain and possibly destabilising change in political relationships which undermines the continuity of the political system?

Commentators have warned of such a possibility. Professor George Winterton stated: 'The most worrisome aspect of a directly elective presidency is that the enhanced authority that will inevitably accrue to that office will destabilise and radically alter Australian government.'[3] Former Labor Minister Barry Jones described a system with an elected Prime Minister and an elected President as 'a car with two steering wheels'.[4] Former Prime Minister John Howard has warned that a directly elected President:

> would alter for all time the nature of our system of government. It would entrench rival centres of political power ... [A]n Australian president, having a popular mandate, would feel infinitely more powerful in dealing with an incumbent Prime Minister than would any Governor-General, irrespective of the formal powers which might be given to that president.[5]

It is believed that the election of a President would open up new possibilities for the abuse of power in office and for the kind of misbehaviour that can lead to constitutional crises. There is a danger, for instance, that the President or Prime Minister would take as his or her chief political objective the perpetuation of his or her own position. The engagement of the two highest political office holders in Machiavellian activities would be not only mischievous but potentially harmful to the stability of the whole political system. How such situations might occur and how they might be avoided are questions of significance worth pondering.[6] In fact there are two good reasons for doing so. First, such Machiavellian moments, for most of us, are outside our lived experience. Most of our institutions, culture, traditions and practices conspire to restrain abuses of power.[7] It is only by imagining constitutional crises that we can comprehend how they might arise. A second reason for addressing such Machiavellian moments is to alert ourselves to the limitations within ourselves and our institutional defences against such abuses of power.[8]

Contemplating such crises also raises the question which is in the background in complex democratic states: When is it appropriate to interrupt the ordinary course of politics in order to maintain political stability and public confidence in government?[9]

The two dismissals discussed earlier in chapter 4 illustrate that crisis is part of Australian constitutional history. While these crises have been rare and Australian government has been stable, the possibility of crisis and political instability cannot be ignored. We need to imagine such crises in order to defend against them. The value of various proposals is to be found in their capacity to forestall such abuses of power. Many republicans have sought to address problems of political instability through crafting legal constraints. This too represents one approach to addressing the issues of contemporary global crises. In relation to terrorism, for instance, quite draconian laws have been enacted.[10]

In this chapter I want to address the issue of crisis by suggesting that we look to the political realm to address the underlying problems.

This is not to downplay the significance of these global challenges but it is to endeavour to find some more subtle ways of political and legal thinking.[11] Law will still have a role to play and will be important, but it must respond to the illegitimacy of political action. We must foster republican solutions to promote the ordinary course of democratic politics.

While I believe that the best way to appoint the head of state is through some form of election, we also need to focus our thinking about the role of the future President. In this chapter, I propose an alternative way of understanding the Australian head of state's role, one which is more practical and more relevant to the functioning of our political system. That is, a conception of the head of state as the guarantor of the continuity of democratic government. But first, it is valuable to consider the implications of the appointment process for political stability.

Implications for political stability

Political stability is fundamental to all functioning democracies. It refers to the orderly transfer from one government to another, and to the ongoing maintenance of the structures of democratic government. The possibility for instability exists in every political system.

This may occur when those in power seek to perpetuate their own position. For example, in the middle of last century, fascist dictators grabbed power in Italy and Germany. More recently, there have been numerous coups in Fiji. These historical moments highlight how such instability imperils democratic government. Contemporary Western democracies are not immune from this concern, even where there is an established pattern of periodic elections or a constitutional requirement for them.[12]

In Australia, instances of political instability have arisen in the context of a conflict between the head of government and the head of state – between the Governor-General and the Prime Minister, or between the Governor and the State Premier.[13] Where there have been constitutional crises, such as the dismissal of the federal Whitlam Government in 1975 and the dismissal of the NSW Lang Government in 1932, they have ultimately been resolved in a democratic manner: for example, through an election.[14] However, they still demonstrate the fragile nature of democratic government.

In resolving a constitutional dispute the head of state is typically charged with deciding either whom to invite to form a government or to dissolve Parliament and allow a fresh election. The instances in which these independent judgments are called for are likely to become more frequent as 'interest-based' politics grows, party loyalties weaken and multi-party parliaments become more common. In fact, the close results in Western Australian (2007), Victorian (1999) and Tasmanian (1989) elections produced minority governments. In these circumstances, the power to select who should govern, and whether those already in power should continue to govern, is critical.

Accordingly, it is valuable to explore how conduct by the head of state could lead to political instability, under both the current system and in a republic. The Prime Minister and Cabinet might seek to continue to govern or to prevent any other leader being given the chance to govern.[15] The Prime Minister might claim an indefinite term in office and resist the intervention of the head of state to call a general election, engaging in a campaign of disparagement of the President's legitimacy. He/she might cast doubt on the President's political even-handedness, or on the right of the President to intrude into the continued working of a 'popularly elected' government. Concerns over such disparagement and over the possibility that the President's orders would be ignored by political leaders are, admittedly, concerns about extreme political situations: they contemplate a Prime Minister who refuses to submit to the direction of the head of state, which would amount to a revolutionary moment.[16]

The President might be tempted to exercise the powers of office for his/her benefit, or may even attempt to arrogate additional powers, or to aggrandise their office.[17] For instance, the President could abandon any deference to the advice of the elected ministry in relation to, say, the dissolution of Parliament, or attempt to exercise independent judgment where his/her role as Governor-General today would simply be formal. They may, for example, refuse to sign executive orders in relation to legislation. The 'potential would exist for the representative and democratically elected parliamentary chambers to be gradually diminished, while the embodiment of the nation and increased powers would be vested in one person'.[18]

Another possibility is that the Prime Minister and the President would join together to perpetuate the government's term of office with the President either acquiescing or, worse, colluding with a request for support from the Prime Minister. The Prime Minister might claim it is in the national interest that he or she continues to govern beyond the set term within which an election must be held. The President, as a figure of national unity and identity, could respond by calling on the people of Australia to unite behind the government in a time of crisis or as a matter of overwhelming necessity. Collusion would take place by the Prime Minister and the President asserting their political and perhaps moral authority.

It is precisely to such potential crises that constitutional safeguards should be directed. Most of the attempts to restrain the actions of the head of government and the head of state have focused on the legality of the actions of both office holders. It is my argument, however, that an equally crucial consideration is the political legality and legitimacy of their actions.

Legality and legitimacy – what is the real issue?

The actions of the Governor-General or President fulfil the requirements of legality if they adhere to the terms of the Constitution and comply with established constitutional practice.[19] The powers of the head of state will be important in resolving a constitutional crisis, but they are not necessarily altered by the shift from a monarchy to a republic. Assuming that the reserve powers of the President will be the same as those of the Governor-General, instances of abuse of power or aggrandisement would infringe the same constitutional principles, whether they were the result of presidential or gubernatorial action. Perpetuating the government's term in office would infringe section 28 of the Constitution, and attempts at aggrandisement contrary to ministerial advice would represent a breach of a constitutional convention. Therefore, identifying the breaches of legal principles advances the analysis of the problem only to a limited extent. We need to think about these problems in other ways. We need to look to political legitimacy to really understand the difference between monarchy and republic.

Legitimacy refers to the rightful source of power from which office holders or institutions in a political system derive their authority.[20] Under the current arrangements, the sources of authority of the Governor-General and the Prime Minister differ. The Prime Minister has a popular constituency (based on election) while the Governor-General, as an appointee of the Prime Minister, has no popular mandate. Instead, the head of state carries an ancient and, in a sense, patriarchal responsibility for preserving the peace and for orderly public authority. In addition, the Governor-General's duty comes from being a representative of the monarch, who has hereditary legitimacy, and from the monarch's special position within the established legal–constitutional order. With the transition to a republic, the President, whether elected directly by the people or by the Parliament, would become another people's representative.

Legitimacy has another vital function: it justifies political action. Democratic legitimacy, based as it is on citizens' participation in the selection of office holders, and office holders' dependence on ongoing public support, operates to justify political action. An elected President would thus offer different justifications and excuses for breaching key constitutional principles than would a Governor-General. Presidents, whether elected by Parliament or by the people, might rely on a populist mandate and republican reasoning to justify their breaches.

The proposed change in the mode of appointment of the head of state will therefore result in different justifications for constitutional breaches and bring about a profound change in the justificatory operation of democratic legitimacy. Following are the various modes of appointment and the implications these modes have for constitutional crises.

An appointed Governor-General

Appointed Governors-General have very little democratic legitimacy because they are not elected or answerable to the people for their actions. The democratic legitimacy of the Governor-General to dismiss the Prime Minister and force a general election is very weak, especially since growing republican sentiment has eroded the monarchical basis of authority in Australia. Thus, the dismissal of Prime Minister Gough Whitlam and the subsequent dissolution of Parliament by Governor-General John Kerr in 1975 were enormously controversial. Despite John Kerr claiming that he had acted legally, his political legitimacy to act as he did was seen as highly questionable.

A President who is elected by the Parliament

A President elected by Parliament enjoys a moderate level of democratic support. The President's democratic legitimacy is enhanced if he/she is elected by a parliamentary supermajority – for example, a two-thirds majority of parliamentary representatives. This mode of appointment would provide the President with a stronger mandate to intervene in politics in times of constitutional crisis, such as in order to prevent an abuse by the Prime Minister of his/her powers.

However, it is arguable that the electorate may view such a President as a mere puppet of Parliament and not the direct representative of the people. Thus, the President may not exercise independent political judgment, or may fail to restrain prime ministerial abuses of power. On the other hand, the parliamentary mode of appointment restricts the President's democratic mandate, attenuating any purported justifications of attempts to enlarge upon his/her position.

A President who is directly elected by the people

A directly elected President enjoys a substantial democratic legitimacy and, as the only directly elected officer in the system, would have a much stronger basis for intervening against a Prime Minister who was acting unconstitutionally. The Prime Minister could not argue that the President's mandate was purely formal.

Nonetheless, it is possible that a President with a popular mandate may attempt to aggrandise his/her position based on that mandate. The President could be subjected to constituent and party pressure to renew his/her term or to intervene in parliamentary affairs. It has been observed that a system of popular election suggests that the President should have large powers – at least in reserve – and that he/she would be justified in exercising such powers.

The different modes of electing the head of state may provide either too strong or too weak a justification for political action by the head of state. Paradoxically, it is important that democratic legitimacy not be used to justify corrupting our fundamental democratic structures. Democratic legitimacy is central to the continuity of our system of government, but it can also undermine it. The President should have a limited mandate, to preserve the democratic process. Such a mandate would command widespread support.

Constitutional constraints

Before outlining a proposed President's mandate, it is beneficial to examine various measures to forestall political destabilisation. Both the Keating Government's proposal and the 1999 Constitutional Convention model recognised that new constitutional powers and constraints would have to be created. Here, we evaluate proposed measures, in terms of their constraint of potential acts of collusion and abuse of power by the Prime Minister and the head of state, based on both legality and legitimacy.

Resisting an abuse of power by the Prime Minister

For a head of state to resist an abuse of power by the Prime Minister a fine balance between constraint and empowerment is required. The head of state needs to be empowered to intervene into partisan politics where necessary. As we have seen, each mode of election creates an imbalance of power. The election of a President by parliamentarians provides a much weaker basis for intervention into politics than popular elections, which may accord too great a power to act independently. Various ways to address these imbalances of power may be identified. Thus, the parliamentary elected head of state's legitimacy may be supplemented by their constitutional powers while a popular head of state's legitimacy may be constrained by limiting their constitutional powers. To appreciate the balance between empowerment and restraint to achieve appropriate legitimacy, it is necessary to understand the proposed mode of election, dismissal and the powers of the head of state.

Proposed methods of removal of the President, for instance, may both enhance or constrain their power. The Keating Government's proposed form of removal (a two-thirds majority vote in a joint sitting of both Houses) would have made it difficult to remove the President, strengthening the President's position to intervene where necessary. This would require strong bipartisan support, except where one party achieves an overwhelming majority in Parliament. Before a President could be dismissed, he or she would have to be found guilty of proven misbehaviour or incapacity. Indeed, the very existence of the grounds of dismissal strengthens the President's mandate because dismissal must be justified according to constitutional criteria. However, the President's position is weakened because it was not proposed that dismissal would be contingent on a specified set of facts, circumstances or conditions in a constitutional provision.

A further limit on the power of a President would be that either House may, by simple majority, initiate a joint sitting to censure or remove the head of state. Nonetheless, the vote required to attain a special majority should result in significant security of tenure that would probably not be unduly diminished by the mechanisms for removal or dismissal.

Conversely, the 1999 referendum model made it easier to dismiss the President, weakening the position of the President from which to intervene where necessary. The Howard Government's Constitutional Convention proposed that:

> The President may be removed at any time by a notice in writing signed by the Prime Minister. The President is removed immediately the Prime Minister's written notice is issued. The Prime Minister's action must be presented to a meeting of the House of Representatives for the purpose of its ratification within 30 days of the date of removal of the President. In the event the House of Representatives does not ratify the Prime Minister's action, the President would not be restored to office, but would be eligible for re-appointment. The vote of

the House would constitute a vote of no confidence in the Prime Minister.[21]

This is a relatively weak form of protection of the President's power, since the Prime Minister's decision only needs to be ratified a month later by majority in the House of Representatives. And as such, it is likely that such a decision would be ratified if the Prime Minister retained the confidence of his or her party prior to the dismissal. Advocates of this model of dismissal thought it appropriate since it was similar to the current power of dismissal vested in the Prime Minister.

Turning from the dismissal procedure to the powers of the President, the basis upon which a head of state could act to resolve a constitutional crisis would also be secured from the substantial 'authority' derived through the current powers of the Governor-General's office. These powers have been seen as sufficient to resolve a constitutional crisis.[22] Not surprisingly, it's been suggested that a future President should possess the constitutional powers presently held by the Governor-General, especially the reserve powers. Finally, the mode of election provides political legitimacy and independence for a directly elected President, and the powers provide a source of limited legitimacy for a parliamentary elected President.

Constraining abuse of power by a President

With the option of vesting the head of state with the current powers of the Governor-General, 'there is a risk that Australian governments may occasionally find themselves in conflict with a head of state who exercises political judgment without regard to the conventions'.[23] This potential for self-aggrandisement exists because of the considerable powers vested in the office, such as in section 61 of the Constitution, which vests executive (governing) power in the Governor-General. The question arises as to how such powers may be subject to an appropriate restraint. One answer is the Constitution should require the head of state to exercise the reserve powers in accordance with existing constitutional conventions. But how can this be achieved? Two options exist. First, constitutional conventions could be retained by way of new provisions referring to the continuity of such conventions. Under this option, the Constitution would not explicitly spell out these conventions. They would be incorporated by reference to their existence.

The failure to include a positive statement of the reserve powers in the Constitution has important implications for abuse of power by the head of state. Constitutional conventions are potentially inadequate constraints, especially if there is a failure to describe their content. The text of the Constitution provides the basis for a future head of state to act independently. Unspecified conventions are not effective counterweights because existing conventions confer on the head of state a broad discretion or may even be ignored. As the Keating Government admitted, a head of state may occasionally exercise political judgment without regard to the conventions.[24] As the head of state also possesses a broad discretion under the reserve powers, he or she may change the ministry to ensure support for his or her point of view.[25]

Codifying the head of state's powers

The second option is to codify the gubernatorial conventions. A code would set out in a special constitutional section the instances in which the President could exercise their judgement. Proponents of a directly elected President often stress that their powers need to be constrained by codification.[26] The non-reserve powers could be spelled out in a straightforward way, such as by providing that the executive powers, vested by section 61, in the head of state are exercised on the advice of the ministry.[27] The codification of the reserve powers is more contentious. And there are two sides to this debate. For codification, it is argued that it:

- is possible to codify the constitutional conventions because these are rules of political practice necessary to confine the discretion of the head of state[28]
- would 'provide certainty and clarity as to the options open to a head of state in different situations'.[29]

Against codification, it is argued that:

- it is impossible to codify the reserve powers because of their nature
- spelling out the reserve powers in a written constitution would petrify them[30] because they would become rigid rules of law
- the reserve powers should continue to be flexible and adaptable.[31]

The partial or full codification of the reserve powers is another contentious issue. Eminent scholar, the late Professor George Winterton resolved the dilemma this way:

> Complete codification would be both inadvisable – because the flexibility necessary for dealing with political crises would be lost – and extremely difficult, if not impossible, because the community is divided on some powers, especially the power to dismiss a Prime Minister denied Supply by the Senate.[32]

Three arguments in favour of partial codification are that:

1. Rules can provide specific guidance for the proper function of government.
2. It is desirable to confine the scope of the head of state's discretion.
3. It would promote clarity and certainty.

The purpose of such a code is to preserve the fundamental constitutional principles of the rule of law and representative and responsible government.[33] The powers of the new head of state would be the bare minimum so as to preserve the continuity of democratic government. If called upon, the President should have the power to initiate a procedure to settle a political impasse by democratic means, such as referring the issue to Parliament or a general election.[34] There is, though, one further problem with a code – inevitable ambiguities, omissions and discretionary space. Such a code would not be complete or exhaustive, and within this discretionary space, questions of democratic legitimacy will arise. In a time of crisis the public will be concerned principally with the preservation of democratic government, not with the technicalities of such a code. One solution to this problem is to provide a simple and straightforward guiding concept, providing justification for political action, a strategy examined in relation to the function of the head of state below.

Preventing collusion

Rules against collusion proscribe legitimate political activity. Collusion may be induced, desired or compelled by necessity. And measures to prevent it may minimise inducement and maximise independence in order to resist claims of necessity. A politically impartial head of state could be created by insulating the President from political allegiance and financial inducement.

There are rules specifically designed to remove inducements. The opportunities for those outside government to influence the head of state by financial inducement would be diminished by the provision of an adequate salary, and by an express prohibition on the president holding any other remunerative position while in office. Other measures that have been suggested could also be taken to insulate the President from financial pressures exerted by the government, such as his or her salary not being subject to income tax or diminished for the entire term. At the expiration of the term the President could be prohibited from receiving remuneration from the Commonwealth in addition to his or her retirement allowance for a period of five years.

If appointed by Parliament, the term of the head of state could be limited to five years, ensuring he or she cannot be influenced by offers to renew the appointment. An appointment for five years is likely to be of sufficient duration to attract qualified candidates and to ensure that the President has a measure of independence from the House of Representatives, which must itself go to the people before the expiration of three years. A single-term presidency is likely to limit collusion between the head of state and the Prime Minister by reinforcing the importance of rotation in office.

Another rule aimed at promoting an impartial head of state and removing partisan allegiances was put forward by former Prime Minister Paul Keating. Keating proposed that serving and former politicians (Commonwealth, State and Territory) would not be eligible for appointment to the office for five years after their departure from politics.[35] The justification for this policy is that the head of state should be politically neutral and impartial, notwithstanding the number of past politicians who have discharged the duties of the office of head of state with distinction.[36] While the head of state obviously ought not to be a Member of Parliament, the effect of the proposed restriction may be to remove suitable candidates. There are other vetting processes that are less restrictive. Selection of the President by a vote of the Parliament is more likely to be an effective method of ensuring that someone either known or expected to be politically partial would not be appointed.[37] In a direct popular election such a disqualification would be an unprecedented restriction on the capacity of citizens to choose their representatives.[38]

Acting on advice of a constitutional council

The head of state's action may be justified if they can show that they acted according to suitable and sound advice. To achieve this, it has been suggested that a Council of Advisors be established 'whose advice must be sought, but not necessarily followed, before a reserve power is exercised without or against ministerial advice'.[39] The virtue of this proposal is that the head of state may receive wise advice, especially since a President may have no experience of government or the law. The proposed Council of Advisors, of perhaps three to five members, would consist of former High Court Justices and former heads of state.[40] It has been further suggested that the advice of the council should not be subject to review by the courts.[41] The problem with such a council is that it is unelected, unaccountable, and will be viewed as an elite body. The advisors may disagree, providing no obvious solution to such a problem. At worst it might compete for power and influence with the President and the Parliament. The council might also call into question the role of the Governor-General or President, should he or she not act on their advice. By appointing these members as councillors their advice is elevated above any other source of advice provided to the head of state, and this is a very great power. While not all consultative councils may be subject to these limitations, we should bear these criticisms in mind when assessing such proposals.

The Governor-General has other options for legal advice: the Commonwealth Solicitor-General, the Attorney-General's Departmental Secretary, retired judges, academics and political scientists. Each of these advisors is quickly contactable via modern communications. The possibility of consulting the Chief Justice of the High Court has now been foreclosed because of the controversy over Chief Justice Barwick's advice in the 1975 crisis. Even if the Governor-General had permission to consult the Chief Justice or a sitting judge it is probably unlikely.

It would also be open to the head of state in a time of political crisis to convene a meeting between the Prime Minister, the Leader of the Opposition and other relevant Members of Parliament. During such a meeting, the head of state would have the opportunity to gain further information, and he or she could also attempt to negotiate a settlement or encourage the parties to resolve the dispute themselves. The Governor-General has many sources of advice that can be drawn upon in a constitutional crisis.

Function of the head of state

Having considered the specific powers that could be conferred on a republican President, it is important to examine the broader issue of the role of the head of state. By role, I mean their constitutional function in a democracy rather than a comprehensive outline of their powers and duties.

Various roles have been suggested but the most common is that he or she is a 'constitutional umpire'[42] who judges and decides a disputed issue. However, ultimately, decisions are not made by the Governor-General but his or her advisors or the people. Thus the analogy of an umpire is incomplete and misleading in terms of describing the functions of the Governor-General.

Some might be further misled that the role of Governor-General is to act as a sports umpire or court. Instead, their function is residual, not as an active judge. Indeed, the principle body employed to resolve legal disputes is the courts.

Yet another function ascribed to the head of state is that of the 'ultimate constitutional guardian to enforce the Constitution and its principles when threatened[43].' A guardian is someone who cares for another or protects or defends them until they can do so for themselves. A President may take on this responsibility and may even enforce constitutional principles. But this definition suggests a more active role for the head of state than is warranted. For instance, what threats should the guardian address and what laws should the guardian enforce?[44] Overall, the guardian role presupposes too proactive a function for the head of state, departing from the norms of our current system.

Yet a third constitutional role, and one preferred, is that the head of state is a guarantor of the continuity of democratic government. This proposal entails re-envisioning the political relationship between the head of state and the Prime Minister. The head of state would be designated as the guarantor of the continuity of democratic government, never as the provider of good government.[45]

The President's role as constitutional guarantor can be explained by way of analogy with a contractual guarantor. A guarantor gives a personal undertaking to remedy any default by a particular contractual party. The role of a guarantor is not to ensure that the contract between the parties is performed well or performed effectively; rather, it is a personal undertaking that in the case of default by one of the parties, he/she will discharge the core obligations of the contract.

The constitutional guarantor undertakes to act when the head of government contravenes a constitutional convention or a term of the Constitution in such a way as to imperil the continuity of democratic government.[46] In such circumstances, the actions of the Prime Minister would amount to a breach of the political contract that exists between the head of government and the people, a compact which requires the Prime Minister to act constitutionally and not to abuse the powers of office.

The President would be permitted to exercise the reserve powers to remove the constitutional threat in the immediate term, discharging his/her personal undertaking. The matter could then be put to the people at the earliest opportunity, through an election. Alternatively, the President may put the matter before Parliament for its consideration. This proposed concept has a number of advantages:

- The concept of constitutional guarantor is meant to be accessible to members of the community, providing them with standards by which to assess and judge the conduct of the President and the Prime Minister.

- The President's expressly stated guarantor function would operate clearly to justify his/her actions to prevent relevant abuses of power by a Prime Minister.
- An express statement of the President's guarantor function would also discourage a President from attempting to usurp a governing role.
- The guarantor function would inhibit collusion, since as guarantor he/she is not a partisan political player.
- The guarantor function may not forestall a premature dismissal but it would frame that debate in terms of the appropriately constrained presidential action.

Yet another advantage of the guarantor notion is that it confers a clear and constitutional function on the head of state, one which takes the head of state outside the political arena. The challenge would be to add this function to the Governor-General's existing role, which is to act on advice, departing from the minimalist model of a republic.

One potential disadvantage of the guarantor function is that it may be too limited. The notion of guarantor might suggest that intervention is only permitted where there is a breach of a constitutional provision or convention. But the function is not so described, nor so limited. Intervention to prevent a potential breach may be permitted, but it could only be justified to preserve the continuity of democratic government. After all, the guarantor is one who provides a guarantee. The head of state must assume responsibility for the continuity of democratic government.[47]

Narrowly defined conceptions of guarantor in the Australian context, if widely disseminated and generally understood, will strengthen political stability and enhance the democratic legitimacy of our system of government.

Conclusion

There are no firm constraints on those empowered through the recognition or creation of high political office. As we have seen, a presidential office (vested with the current reserve powers of the Governor-General) will not be sufficient to prevent or resolve any constitutional crises. Such a resolution does not merely consist of compliance with the legal requirements of the reserve powers. However, there are conceptions of legitimate power which, when expressed in the constitutional text, will control the excesses of office holders. Thus, the concept of legitimacy will play the vital role in both limiting and justifying the powers and actions of an elected President. Various constitutional requirements may forestall illegitimate political action, such as an appropriate mechanism to appoint and remove a President; prescribing and limiting presidential powers; limiting the term of the office and preventing the President from holding another office.

When thinking about republican reform, we must not only see the Constitution as prescribing a set of legal rules, but as establishing political relationships and expressing fundamental values. We must imagine the normalised relationships and appropriate roles of the governors, which are conducive to maintaining political stability. By clearly defining the President's role we can allay many fears, strengthen the democratic safeguards built into our Constitution and build a solid republican consensus. The guarantor notion would both empower the President to restrain an abuse of power by a Prime Minister and limit the President's capacity to usurp a governing role.

This chapter has considered how to create a new stable office of head of state, focusing on maintaining the current powers of the Governor-General but adapting those to a future Australian republic. This approach draws upon the current monarchical structures, infusing them with republican aspirations. An alternative approach might be to abandon our current monarchical structures and conceive of new constitutional provisions for a republican head of state.[48] It would entail identifying what we would 'like a head of state to do under an Australian republic' and 'try and construct a constitution that is more explicit about how it works'.[49] The guarantor function, in this context, might provide a useful guide for the establishment of a re-imagined head of state.[50] While this is an ambitious task, it is one that we may have to think about sooner rather than later.

Beyond establishing conceptions of legitimate constitutional power, it must be borne in mind that great care is required for constitutional adjustment, as changes in the structure of the constitutional order will invariably lead to changes in power, in the behaviour of those in public office and, ultimately, in the sense of political responsibility within the whole citizenry.

8

Ask the leaders and the people

What were the views of the leaders and what were the views of the people regarding the 1999 referendum debate? To find out the views of voters about the issues surrounding the 1999 republic referendum, researchers Gow, Bean and McAllister surveyed thousands of Australians. This survey is well known to political scientists, less well known to constitutional lawyers, and even less well known to the general public. But it does provide some fascinating information. In 2008–09, I interviewed some key leaders in the 1999 referendum campaign and found it interesting to compare the leader's views with those of the voters. I wanted to know what the most popular arguments were and the reasons why the 1999 referendum failed.

To find my answers I drew on three sources: the Yes/No pamphlet, containing arguments for and against the referendum question, posted to each elector;[1] the leaders' views, then and now, as drawn from news reports, books and my interviews; and the *Australian Constitutional Referendum Study 1999* (the '1999 survey').[2]

It is important to note that in drawing on some sources, it can be difficult to ascertain which arguments were most influential. The way people cast their vote was determined by the interplay of different arguments and associations. Thus, the expert opinion data collected from the interviews provides a way to assess the influence of arguments on different voting groups. Yet another difficulty is that the 1999 survey did not ask questions based on the arguments in the Yes/No pamphlet, although the survey questions were framed to be consistent with that document.[3] While the survey was 'representative of the opinions of the people at large',[4] a further difficulty is that the questions in the survey are rather brief, limiting the information we can draw from them. There are also some issues and arguments on which we do not have any survey data.

Despite this, the 1999 survey provides data about a range of arguments put to the people including those invoking nationalist sentiment, drumming up support for and against the status quo, and debating the merits of the proposed republican model. It also covers people's opinions on other factors or associations, such as party loyalty, religion, gender, age, education and knowledge of the Constitution. The survey also provides us with the opportunity to reflect upon what may move the electorate to adopt a republican form of government in a future referendum.

Arguments

Amongst the important arguments put to Australian voters at the 1999 referendum were the following:

- An Australian should be our head of state.
- Australia should retain our current system of government: the Governor-General and State Governors.
- Those who don't know – vote 'No'.
- Voters should vote 'No' to the politician's republic.
- Those who want to elect their President should vote 'No'.
- There will be no benefits under this republic – only problems.

An Australian should be our head of state

The Yes campaign message that an Australian should be Australia's head of state is a view that had popular support. Yes campaigner Professor Greg Craven explained the logic of the argument: because we have '… the Australian Constitution, we should have an Australian head of state, it's entirely logical … why on earth would you want a hereditary head of state? It's inconsistent'.[5] For former Leader of the Opposition Kim Beazley the argument was 'essentially [about] symbols, because Australia is an independent nation, now out of any colonial embrace ... it should appoint its own head of state'.[6] John Howard agreed: '[T]he only decent argument the republicans had was that we shouldn't share our legal head of state or sovereign with other countries.[7]

The 1999 referendum survey supported the leaders' views. Overall, 88.9 per cent of respondents to the 1999 survey 'agreed' or 'strongly agreed' that our head of state should be an Australian.[8] This view is reinforced by the findings of the 1999 survey that 65.4 per cent of respondents believed that the Queen and the Royal Family were 'not very important' to Australia.[9] Accordingly, the No case decision not to mention the Queen was justified by her marginal relevance to debate. We can see then that the landscape of Australian politics had changed by the 1999 referendum. Although the clarion call for an Australian head of state had a strong nationalist appeal and support, other arguments and influences conspired to defeat the referendum.

Australia should retain our current system of government: the Governor-General and State Governors

This argument expressed a preference for the status quo over the republican model offered. It was premised on the view that there were insufficient reasons given to alter the current system.[10] The No campaign relied upon the classic status quo argument that 'If it ain't broke, don't fix it', maintaining that the current system is both certain and stable, and that Australians ought not to 'allow our tried and proven Constitution to be replaced by an experiment'.[11] A change to the system would be 'an experiment with unknown disastrous consequences'.[12] It is worth emphasising, though, that the No case did not mention the role of the Queen, downplayed the role of the Governor-General and did not mention the State Governors. The tenor of the No case emphasised our current constitutional system of government per se. While many leaders saw this argument as influential, there were some reservations expressed regarding the importance of this point.

Former Prime Minister John Howard's view was that the referendum 'failed because of the inherent unwillingness on the part of Australians to change something that they haven't been persuaded was no longer working. This is the number one reason'.[13] Direct electionist Phil Cleary agreed, but gave it a different weight: '[conservatism] did play a role because it was part of the No vote ...'[14]

Yes campaigner and Australian Republic Movement Chairman Malcolm Turnbull also spoke of a 'natural conservatism' – 'the system works well, why change it?'[15] And Executive Director for Australians for Constitutional Monarchy Kerry Jones agreed: 'Well it's a great

Constitution, it's served Australia very well.'[16] Sir David Smith suggested: 'We have been given no good reasons for removing the Crown.'[17] Supporters of the Australian Constitution and the Constitutional Monarchists saw the status quo argument as the most influential. Republicans saw it as less important.

The 1999 survey did not ask questions about the role of our constitutional system. Rather, it asked about people's support for the current system of representative democracy. This kind of argument lends support to the No case, presumably if we can make the connection that the Constitution supports our democratic system. Most people were 'very' or 'fairly' proud of the way democracy works in Australia (77.2 per cent of respondents).[18] Pride in Australian democracy also exhibited in the respondents' support for the process of voting.

The survey asked if whom you vote for makes a difference. Over 60 per cent of respondents agreed with this proposition; an argument based on support for the current institutions of Australian democracy had a good deal of popular appeal. However, the criticism that the 1999 model endangered our political stability was less effective. Only 23.7 per cent of respondents agreed or strongly agreed that Australia's record of political stability would be endangered if Australia was to become a republic, in contrast to nearly 35 per cent who neither agreed nor disagreed and around 40 per cent who disagreed or strongly disagreed.[19] Interestingly, only 45.1 per cent of people voted in favour of a republic in the 1999 referendum. The strength of the No case, then, may have been the appeal to the lack of voter knowledge.

Those who don't know – vote 'No'

While there was considerable support for the workings of Australian democracy there was apparently insufficient knowledge regarding the Australian Constitution and the details of the proposed model. This raises the question: are these responses contradictory? How can one believe in the system of democracy but not know about the workings of the Constitution? It is, of course, possible for the general public to be aware of the workings of Australian democracy. After all, this is visible on television every night and the public regularly vote in compulsory elections. Understanding the details of the Australian Constitution and the workings of the proposed bipartisan model is a different point altogether.

The No case relied upon voters' lack of knowledge: 'Those who don't know – should vote "NO" – because that is the only safe way to go.'[20] Two issues emerge here: lack of understanding of the current system and of the proposed alternative model. At the time of the referendum, for Malcolm Turnbull, the most influential argument against the republic was based on the voter's lack of understanding:

> Ignorance was the Republic's greatest enemy, though we republicans have been branded sore losers for

saying as much ... Anyone who understands the system of government we have is almost certainly a supporter of the bipartisan model. The problem is that hardly anyone understands our system of government.[21]

The assumption that underlies Turnbull's view is that, with proper education, voters would support the bipartisan model. There is some evidence to support the view that education may change voting preferences, but not necessarily formal education. Of course acceptance does not arise automatically from understanding.

Nonetheless, survey data indicates that the Australian people are ill-informed about the Australian constitutional system. For instance, a survey collected by the Constitutional Commission in 1987 found that just under half of those surveyed were not aware that Australia even had a written Constitution.[22] Furthermore, The Civics Expert Group 1994 Survey found that 'only 18 per cent [of Australians] know something about the content of the Constitution'.[23] People may be relatively uninformed about the Australian Constitution for a variety of reasons, including:

- The Constitution is a reasonably long and technical document.
- Many constitutional provisions regulate government and are not directly relevant to the lives of ordinary people.

- The Constitution does not feature in media reports on a daily basis.

Periodically, an issue may arise, like the 1975 Australian constitutional crisis, which makes the Constitution of interest to the general public. At most other times, the Australian Constitution's accomplishment of its purpose to provide stable government means that the media has no need to be interested in our founding document at all.

We might speculate that voters would vote against the republic because they believe the current Australian system works well and they consequently have no need to be interested in changing it. Kerry Jones saw it this way: 'A related reason for defeat was that the people failed to understand the alternative model.'[24] Malcolm Turnbull also saw this as a significant problem: 'The simple fact is that the referendum was defeated in large measure because many people misapprehended the nature and consequences of the change.'[25]

Professor Greg Craven, Yes campaigner, confronted some 'extremely unflattering arguments' against the proposal based on voter ignorance. 'The two arguments that I constantly encountered were; [First] there are [67] amendments to the Constitution … it must be a disaster … [second] we were going to be thrown out of the Commonwealth Games.'[26]

Professor Craven remarked that if 'these sceptics had read about the changes they would have recognised that most of the changes to the Constitution were simply changing Governor-General to President'.[27] The concern over the Commonwealth Games is significant in that it reflects a misunderstanding about the ties between Australia, Britain and the Commonwealth. Although his comment is telling about the national attachment to sporting endeavours, it was also an issue specifically addressed by the Yes campaign in literature distributed to every household. That sort of anecdote speaks volumes about the efficacy of education. You can post out pamphlets, but people have to care enough to read them.

The 1999 referendum survey indicated that there were various misunderstandings about the proposed changes to the Constitution. Many respondents were mistaken about how the change would affect ties between Britain and Australia. While over 88 per cent of people supported an Australian head of state, there was a fairly even split (40 per cent in favour and 40 per cent against) about keeping constitutional ties with Britain.[28] Under the republic proposal it would be impossible to keep the Queen as the principal constitutional tie yet have an Australian head of state.

Respondents also exhibited a lack of knowledge about the model itself. Nearly 70 per cent of respondents either didn't know or misunderstood how the President could be dismissed under the bipartisan model.[29] We should not be surprised by some of these misunderstandings since in the Yes case pamphlet the working of the model was not comprehensively described. A lay person may have been able to divine the workings of the model from the constitutional amendments also distributed, but for most this would have been a daunting task. As Ian McAllister remarked, the referendum involved a 'highly technical choice'.[30] By contrast, the No case criticised features of the model, maintaining that:

> Those who want an appointed President – should vote 'NO' – because the proposed model is fatally flawed. The President will be a Prime Minister's puppet, subject to instant dismissal.[31]

Thus the No case focused on a particular aspect of the referendum model, the Prime Minister's power to dismiss the President.[32] Criticisms of the dismissal feature might plausibly have influenced people's decision because they were emphasised by the No campaign to undermine the Yes case in favour of the republic.

Vote 'No' to the politician's republic

The No campaign in the referendum maintained that the parliamentary elected model was the 'Politician's Republic'.[33] Many leaders shared this view. Direct electionist Phil Cleary recalled a 'reservoir ... of opposition to the idea of politicians electing the president'.[34] Australians for Constitutional Monarchy Executive Director Kerry Jones said the referendum model 'focused more power on politicians in Australia'.[35]

This argument emphasised the negative perceptions of politicians, which was borne out by the 1999 survey. Over 60 per cent of survey respondents thought politicians 'usually' or 'sometimes' looked only after themselves, and around 60 per cent of respondents thought that politicians did not know what 'ordinary people' thought.[36] Many of the respondents had negative perceptions; criticisms such as the politician's republic would appeal to those views. Thus, the survey data also indicates a limit to how nuanced the public debate might be between the merits of a direct and an indirect election model, particularly given the intention to maintain the Westminster system with a politically neutral head of state.

Those who want to elect their President should vote 'No'

The No case proposed that '[t]hose who want to elect their President – should vote "No" – because under the proposed model, they will have no say in who their President will be'.[37] Many of the leaders saw this argument as influential.

Liberal Member Bob Charles put it this way: 'I don't think the public is ever going to get excited about a parliamentary model. They want an elected President if we're going to have one.'[38] Kim Beazley believed that '[t]he Australian people will not vote for a republic unless they are going to be directly involved in electing the head of state'. He also recognised a concern, at the time, that '[i]f we put in place [a parliamentary elected] model we'll never get an elected presidency'.[39]

Phil Cleary maintained, 'the only model that will be accepted by the people is one in which the President is elected'.[40]

These leaders believed that the direct election argument influenced people not to vote for parliamentary election because of the popular appeal of the vote. There was also a fear that the electors would not get a chance to vote for a directly elected President in the future if the 1999 referendum model was successful.

The survey data showed strong support for a directly elected President with: 54 per cent of the respondents supporting a President by direct election, 20 per cent supporting a President by parliamentary election and 24 per cent supporting retention of the monarchy.[41] What is striking about these findings is the strength of support for a directly elected head of state. Direct electionist republicans have argued that the model that most people want is the one that ought be put to the people.[42] Support for this view may be found in the number of republicans who 'voted "yes", but preferred a directly elected head of state', estimated at '31% of the total electorate'.[43]

Consideration must also be given to the disparity between the survey data and the result of the referendum. At the referendum 45.1 per cent voted in favour of the republic, suggesting that perhaps some people in favour of direct election were prepared to support a parliamentary elected head of state. This is not surprising given the strong support generally for appointing an Australian citizen as our head of state. The question remains to what extent a parliamentary model could gain additional votes to achieve a majority. Conversely, a direct election model may be more likely to receive first and second preferences amounting to a majority. John Pike's analysis of the 1999 survey estimates that a direct election model would have received a vote of between 64 and 71 per cent.[44] The question remains to what extent such majority support for a direct election model will withstand public scrutiny and criticism. In considering any future republican mode of selection, opinions will differ over their popular appeal.

There will be no benefits under this republic – only problems

The No case argued that the republic 'won't create jobs … improve trade …. the economy or our lives'.[45] The 1999 survey addressed this issue less directly by asking if respondents believed that the whole debate over Australia becoming a republic was a distraction from Australia's real problems. Fifty per cent of the respondents agreed, 19.6 per cent were undecided, and 27 per cent disagreed.[46] The difficulty of assessing the distraction argument is that the question was a leading one – suggesting a diminished importance of the republic. Nonetheless, it may be that the issue didn't influence voters' preferences, since 89 per cent agreed that Australia should have its own head of state.[47]

Such a high consensus is not easy to achieve and presumably attests to the importance of the issue. Alternatively, the responses illustrate the complexity of people's beliefs: a capacity to hold in one's mind two competing opinions, one a criticism of the debate and the other a preference for a republic.

Given the complex range of arguments involved, individual votes cast for or against the republic was the result of a combination of beliefs and judgements. We have some information about these underlying reasons: support for a republic, regard for the status quo, distrust of politicians, ignorance of the Constitution and the alternative model. We need also to consider other factors associated with the voters' decisions.

Associations

Although voters were influenced by arguments about the republic, a number of independent political and social factors were associated with their decision making too. These include personal characteristics and beliefs. Researchers have identified the social and political bases of republican voting drawing upon the 1999 survey. Many of these bases are independent and not directly related to republican arguments. Three bases that should be considered are:

1 political leaders and parties;
2 personal characteristics, values and beliefs; and
3 level of education.

It is important to emphasise that, statistically speaking, substantive issues such as support for the status quo, or the benefits of the republic, were more determinative of voters' choices than many of their personal characteristics or beliefs.[48]

Political leaders and parties

How much did the personal popularity of the leaders influence the outcome of the referendum? Here 'popularity' refers to the popularity of the leader, not their message. Was the popularity of the mainstream political leaders most influential? Professor Clive Bean has researched this very issue, and argues that the 1999 survey indicates that Prime Minister Howard's personal image had little or no influence on how people voted for a republican head of state; whereas Kim Beazley's popularity resulted in a significant yet still relatively modest increase in support for the republic.[49] While this may sound like a surprising result to many, owing to the criticism that John Howard's actions contributed to the failure of the referendum, it is important to recognise the narrow focus of the research, which examined only popularity, not the Prime Minister's lack of support for the proposal. Many believe that a referendum cannot succeed without the support of the Prime Minister.[50]

Other republican and monarchist politicians did have a marginal influence on the debate,[51] probably because the focus during the campaign was on the respective campaign leaders rather than the Prime Minister or Opposition Leader.[52] Kerry Jones, of Australians for Constitutional Monarchy, increased the popularity of the No case, whereas Malcolm Turnbull decreased the popularity of the Yes case.[53] It should be noted that the focus of Bean's analysis was not on the respective leaders' leadership per se, but rather their personal popularity. Thus leaders' popularity did have a minimal impact on how people voted, but it was not the central issue.

The history of referendums suggests that they fail unless there is a concerted bipartisan campaign in favour of the proposition by the major parties.[54] The 1999 republic referendum was unusual in that the governing Liberal Party neither opposed nor supported the proposal. The Liberal Party adopted a neutral position because of differences of opinion within their ranks. McAllister has argued that there were no clear partisan cues to guide electors in making their decision in the republic referendum.[55] However, according to McAllister, the absence of partisanship led to de facto opposition between the political parties on the republic issue. Survey evidence suggests people voted Yes or No because of partisan support: most Liberals voted No as monarchists, most Australian Labor Party (ALP) supporters voted Yes as pragmatists.[56] Children of ALP parents were more likely to vote 'Yes' than those of Coalition parents. However, 'Coalition children' were more likely to approve of a Parliament elected head of state, over 'Labor children'.[57] The research suggests that referendum proposals will be defeated if there is opposition or neutrality adopted by the political parties. The 1999 survey supports the need for bipartisan support for a successful referendum campaign.

Personal characteristics, values and belief

Votes were also cast in accordance with a range of independent characteristics including education, gender, age, family circumstances and religion. The voters' political beliefs and orientation, as well as their values and level of trust in politicians, were also important. Dr Bruce Tranter, drawing upon the 1999 survey, has analysed these characteristics and beliefs, and his findings may be summarised in the following:[58]

- Younger generations were more supportive of a President than pre-World War II generations (approximately 2:1).[59]
- Professionals were more likely to vote for a republic than other occupational groups.
- Government employees were slightly more likely than non-government employees to vote 'Yes'.
- Yes voters tended to be secular and lived in large cities.
- More Anglicans were No voters than any other religious group.
- No voters were more likely to have been born in

the United Kingdom or elsewhere (than Australia).
- Men were more likely than women to support either republican model, reflecting a view that the Queen is seen by women as important.
- Political ideology had an impact on voting – the 'Left' more in favour of the republic than the 'Right', 'reflecting the ideological alignment of the major parties'.
- Political leaders provided an important 'lead' for voters.
- Those who trusted politicians were more likely to vote 'Yes'.[60]

Tranter argues that the lack of trust represents 'a degree of cynicism towards politicians ... [and] may also signal preferences for "participatory" democracy, characteristic of new social movement supporters'.[61]

These independent factors indicate the cultural trends between republican and non-republican voters. The trends varied between the city and bush, men and women, and professionals and the middle and working classes. The choices adopted by Anglicans and other religious groups, and the differences between Left and Right are also worth noting. While it may be a little strong to adopt a phrase from the period, the 'culture wars' apparently played a role in the outcome of the referendum.

Levels of education

In what way were voters' levels of education associated with their voting? The trend was such that people with higher levels of formal education were more likely to vote in favour of the republic than those with comparatively lower levels of education. University graduates were twice as likely to vote 'Yes' as the non-tertiary educated.[62] However, such support may be misleading. A high level of education may not necessarily correlate with an informed opinion on political matters. Not everyone with tertiary education (a degree) is interested in such matters, and people without tertiary education are not necessarily disinterested or uninformed.[63] The 1999 survey results showed that the likelihood of voting 'Yes' increased with an individual's interest in politics.[64] Therefore, education may be a crude measure: substituted for a person's level of political knowledge or ability to understand political issues. It may also be that the better a person understands the political debate, the less likely they are to be afraid of changing the Constitution. Tranter makes a similar point in summing up the correct responses to five questions in the 1999 survey dealing with knowledge of the proposed and existing head of state. He shows that '[t]hose who answered all questions correctly were more than three times as likely as those who answered all questions incorrectly to vote "Yes"'.[65]

It has also been argued that if a person is better

informed this may change their vote. In a deliberative poll people were informed about the model and the possible implications, and this changed many of the participants' views from favouring a direct election to supporting a parliamentary elected head of state.[66] Two issues can be drawn from the deliberative poll – the people need to be informed, but also engaged in the debate. In sum, it's not that more highly educated people voted for the republic, it's those who were politically aware.

Reflections on the survey and the future

It is worth pausing to reflect upon the data and the future prospects of an Australian republic. The republic provides us with a paradox: 88 per cent of respondents supported an Australian head of state, yet only 45.1 per cent of votes at the referendum were cast in favour of the republic. However, this finding does not diminish the validity of the survey since the survey data is generally representative. The survey data helps us understand the apparent contradiction; it highlights the complex interplay of different arguments and associations influencing the way people voted. We can also better understand voting patterns by drawing on the expert opinion data collected from the interviews.

The leaders expressed differing views about the failure of the referendum, which appeared to depend upon their position in the debate. Leaders accorded priority to different arguments, and the following illustrates their points of view:

- Advocates of the 1999 referendum model saw the failure as due to lack of voter understanding.
- Direct electionists saw the failure as due to the absence of a popular vote for the President.
- Constitutional monarchists believed that the failure was due to support for the status quo.
- Almost all leaders believe that the proposition, Australia should have its own head of state, was a strong argument for the republic.

Turning from the views of the leaders to the views of the people, the 1999 survey data indicates numerous possible reasons for the failure of the campaign:

- suspicions of politicians
- lack of bipartisan support
- preference for the status quo
- preference for a directly elected over a parliamentary elected President
- lack of knowledge of the Australian Constitution.

From the survey data and the views of the leaders we can make some observations about the strategies and arguments for the future. The responses suggest that we cannot rely on only one strategic change, such as offering a direct election model. Rather, a multifaceted approach needs to be pursued to successfully introduce an Australian republic.

Republican strategy ought to rely on two important arguments: that an Australian should be our head of state and that a new republican model will be more democratic. Even though Australians distrust their politicians, they are overwhelmingly proud of the way democracy works in Australia. While the criticism that the 1999 model endangered our political stability was not that effective, convincing only 23.7 per cent of respondents, 35 per cent of voters were still undecided. Thus the argument that a new model is politically stable will need to be made more convincingly.

The public debate will again focus on the choice between a popular or parliamentary election of the head of state. Voters do take cues from their political leaders, so bipartisan support will be crucial for the success of a republican referendum.

The distraction argument may be more influential the longer the republic campaign continues, so voter education is likely to be vital for an informed debate – even though it may sway some people away from support for direct election to parliamentary election. The workings, though not necessarily the detail of the model, will also need to be widely understood. The Yes case failed to explain this in their arguments and is a plausible reason for voter ignorance of the model. The critical finding from the survey is that the politically aware will be more likely to vote 'Yes'.

We now know the groups (or associations) who voted 'No', and republicans can direct our campaign to addressing their concerns. Success will likely depend upon the way an education campaign engages the people with the issue of the republic.

Perhaps we need a new way of thinking about the republican debate. It is worth pausing to reflect upon what issues are most important to Australians and what we are most proud of. And in this the 1999 referendum survey is highly instructive. Of those surveyed 77 per cent were 'very' or 'fairly' proud of the way democracy works in Australia.[67] This is a high figure. But an even larger number – 95.5 per cent of Australians – were 'very proud' or 'fairly proud' of our achievements in sport.[68] If in public debate rival political camps can be analogised to rival sporting teams, and the constitutional referendum to a sporting contest, then Australia has a sporting chance of becoming a republic.

9

The incurable republic

It has been said that scepticism is a condition of our times. There is a distrust of the propriety of politicians and there is scepticism of grand political narratives.[1] The international failures of confidence that sparked the Global Financial Crisis have challenged the claimed virtues of capitalism. There is even a deep uncertainty about our ability to achieve our goals. And the republic is not immune from this uncertainty. How could the failure of the referendum have not cast a dark pall over the immediate future of Australian republicanism? Failure may well limit the opportunities for renewal, but failure also provides fertile ground for remaking the future.

So in the midst of doubt, how should republicans

respond? When we fail, it is only natural to grieve. But we've had our decade of mourning. It's time to revisit the failures; reflect and work through the challenges. We should return to the wonder of what is possible and chart a future direction for ourselves. This book has been devoted, then, to the ongoing project of political renewal and the re-imagining of the republic. When we imagine, we conjure up an alternative vision, which may inspire but does not necessarily overcome the stumbling block of doubt itself.

We can respond to doubt in a number of ways. First, we ought to begin by believing in ourselves as republicans. We ought to be optimists; perhaps some would say we need to be (incurable) romantics![2] Republicans have certainly been moved by a romantic vision of change. Re-reading the 1999 Yes case, one is struck by its love of country, history, culture and destiny. Unlike the typical Yes/No case pamphlets of the past, the Yes case did not attempt to score points through derision. Rather, it proclaimed an ideal vision. It expressed a desire for 'an aspirational, positive change'.[3] Republicans should continue to be optimists, even romantics, for it is a strength. Kim Beazley summed this up well when he said that a future republic is 'unlikely to succeed unless it's in the hands of a person who loves it'.[4] Republican gatherings and meetings today are still imbued with the vision, but idealism alone does not bring about change. We need more than optimism, even though this ought to be our outlook.

Republic romanticism was not enough to achieve a republic at the last referendum, since it did not necessarily answer two telling criticisms. In the 1999 campaign the critics' arguments resembled two themes that reoccur in debates over reform of institutions and societies: things could be better or they could be worse.[5] On the one hand, critics argued that we would have a better future if we were to elect our President. On the other hand our future would be worse because the bipartisan proposal would be less stable – a flawed dismissal procedure, a sham consultation process and a politicians' republic.

Admittedly, the Yes case did address some criticism that the future republic would be worse than the current system. However, a call to patriotism was not an answer to the rhetoric marshalled by the agents of resistance. Perhaps the key lesson for republicans, whether they favour parliamentary or popular appointment, is the crucial importance of addressing directly the criticism. Doubt can only be addressed when it can be wisely and then confidently dispelled. Republicans, then, need 'a sort of attentiveness and conscientiousness' to the gaps, the point-scoring and the half-truths that precede the failure of a political proposal.[6] People do care about Australia's political future and they do understand the criticisms of a reform proposal. Thus republicans should nurture trust and understanding in the face of doubts which can be easily cast.

A third response to doubt is to make a case for the

model, not just for the change – an argument that moves beyond symbols, sentimentality and optimism. The popular, perhaps the larrikin, and the practical must inform the debate. The realpolitik of change must be explained so knowledge may therefore dispel doubts about the workability of the model. While people don't need to know the minute detail they do need to know about the viability of a proposal. After all, it will be the politically aware who will support a republic. Given how little the people know of the Australian Constitution, a revived republican debate provides opportunities for civic education. This is not only necessary, but desirable.

But what model should Australia adopt for a future republic? This must be the subject of a renewed debate. The appropriate model will only be chosen by a fair and rigorous deliberation of the options, and their strengths and weaknesses must be considered. In that regard, some of the important issues that have been outlined in this book include: defining the mandate of the President, codifying the reserve powers (at least partially), settling on a mode of appointment (either parliamentary or popular), and choosing a method of dismissal. These are the practicalities of change.

In this book I have taken a stand on the appropriate republican reform. I have proposed the retention of a non-executive head of state. I have also suggested a new mandate for the head of state as the constitutional guarantor for the continuity of democratic government. Further, there are important lessons to be drawn from the failure of the 1999 referendum. We must re-engage the people in re-imagining the republic. The people's involvement must lie at the heart of a revived republican reform where the people are engaged with each of the steps for altering the Constitution. The critical steps include an initiation of proposals, selection of a model, informing the people and the formal process of constitutional amendment.

Minimalism's greatest strength was its similarity to the current system; its greatest weakness was the failure to admit the potential for popular political change. No longer should we put our faith in minimalist arguments. Minimalism has ultimately acted as an impediment to debate and imagining a new republican future for ourselves. It is time to open the debate up to other perspectives. We should consider the range of options for a non-executive head of state, which may not adhere in an identical way to the current monarchical system.

The difference between a monarchy and a republic is not to be found simply in the textual changes in the Constitution. Rather, it is to be found in the way in which we confer political legitimacy on a President and their mandate. The test for any future proposal must be judged by three important values: neutrality, political stability and popular participation. These are often not at the forefront of the debate, but ought to guide our considerations in the future.

Under the current Australian Constitution, the

provisions dealing with the powers of the Governor-General do not mean quite what they say. This is in part based on the inheritance of the British monarchy. In a future republican Constitution we must say what we mean, for clarity will bring certainty and stability.

What then are the options for citizens to engage in the republican debate? Some might only wish to vote in a plebiscite or at a referendum. Some might want to convince members of their family to support a republic. Others might wish to join a civic-minded republican organisation.[7] Members of major political parties might also wish to participate and support their parties' republican initiatives. Republicans may wish to support the campaigns of republican leaders and groups. When the republican debate is again at the forefront of our politics, citizens may wish to inform themselves of the issues, take an interest in the media reports and engage with the leaders of the republican debate.

What should the role of our parliamentary leaders be in a future republican discussion? Kevin Rudd and Malcolm Turnbull have declared themselves to be republicans. Each, though, are apparently reluctant republicans as neither has yet made the republic a priority. The adverse economic consequences of the Global Financial Crisis have taken centre stage, and no one ought doubt the seriousness of the current economic climate. But politics is more than economics: there are a kaleidoscope of issues that confront our daily lives. This crisis, like others before it, will pass.

Perhaps, what we need, right now, is some '"un-crisis" thinking – the flip side of crisis thinking'.[8] The thinking associated with 9/11, the Global Financial Crisis and climate change has pushed the republic off the political agenda. Even so, it is still on the map.[9]

The republican ideal still provides the foot-holds for changed governance. We need to revive the 'important relationship between politics (life) and law'.[10] The republic needs to be returned to the 'more inclusive democratic and deliberative processes' of ordinary politics.[11] There is no reason to think that indeed the debate should not begin now – after all, 89 per cent of respondents in the 1999 Australian referendum survey believed that Australia should have its own head of state.[12] Senator Bob Brown from the Greens has commendably taken the initiative, introducing a Bill into the Senate proposing a plebiscite process for a future republic.[13] Republicans must be determined and active in developing the agenda for change, for we believe in something greater than ourselves and the times in which we live, an ideal that will ultimately unify the country.

What then should be our expectations of our political leaders? We should expect our leaders to inspire us. This is not simply asking them to deliver a great speech, although this too will be important. Rather, we ought to expect them to inspire us through their actions. Should we not ask them to be true patriots, to stand up for their convictions? Both Mr Rudd and Mr Turnbull have broadly agreed that the republic ought to be a bipartisan issue. Mr Rudd has said that a republican referendum will only be successful on a 'bipartisan basis',[14] while Mr Turnbull has said he does not want to use the 'republican issue for political advantage'.[15]

Our leaders ought to work towards a bipartisan approach. They ought to agree on a framework for the development of a viable proposal for a republic. The framework should allow time for widespread public consultation and education, and eventually a referendum, and permit productive disagreement even between the political leaders over the desirability of various models. But ultimately, the framework should allow the leaders to reach an agreement to support the referendum proposal.

What will inspire us is, I believe, our leader's commitment to bipartisanship. Indeed, for many this may not seem a particularly inspiring proposal, but the strictures and rigours of partisan politics place great constraints on our leaders. A bipartisan approach may be difficult to achieve in the current tradition of oppositional politics, but we should ask no less of them.

Notes

Introduction

1. Some of them were: former Prime Minister Paul Keating, former Leader of the Opposition Kim Beazley, former Australian Republican Movement Chairman Malcolm Turnbull, former ALP Senator Nick Bolkus, Liberal Senator Marise Payne, former Liberal Member of Parliament Bob Charles, and delegate to the 1998 Constitutional Convention Jason Yat-sen Li.
2. Some of them were: former Prime Minister John Howard, former Executive Director of Australians for Constitutional Monarchy Kerry Jones, Direct Electionist Phil Cleary, and Monarchist Sir David Smith.
3. In a *Bulletin* poll of February 1998, 65 per cent to 24 per cent favoured retaining the Australian over the American system of government. (*The Bulletin*, 17 February 1998, p. 23.) For earlier poll statistics see G Winterton (1993) 'Presidential Power in Republican Australia', *Australian Journal of Political Science*, vol. 28, pp. 40–2.
4. Social Research Centre (2008) *Public Opinion Towards Governance: Results from the Inaugural ANU Poll*, Australian National University, April.
5. Australian Constitution s 128.
6. As Professor Orr notes: 'Terminology is often loosely used in this area.' Orr defines a 'referendum' ... '[as] a binding poll: one that is a necessary part of some legislative or constitutional process'. Conversely, he employs the term 'plebiscite' 'for a poll that is essentially indicative only'. See (2000) 'The conduct of referenda and

plebiscites in Australia: a legal perspective', *Public Law Review*, vol. 11, p. 117.
7   Australian Constitution ss 7 & 24.
8   Australian Constitution s 64; according to constitutional convention, the Governor-General appoints Ministers who have the support of a majority of members who sit in the lower House of Parliament.
9   HB Mayo (1960) 'The Theory of Democracy Outlined' in *An Introduction to Democracy*, Oxford University Press, p. 62.
10 See Australian Constitution s 128; *Attorney-General of the Commonwealth; ex rel McKinlay v The Commonwealth* (1975) 135 CLR 1; *McGinty v Western Australia* (1996) 186 CLR 140; *Mulholland v Australian Electoral Commission* (2004) 220 CLR 181. E Arcioni (2009) 'The vague but powerful abstraction: the concept of "the people" in the Constitution', Paper presented at Gilbert & Tobin Constitutional Law Conference, University of New South Wales, 20 February.
11 See *Singh v Commonwealth* (2004) 222 CLR 322 at [133] per J McHugh dissenting. See E Arcioni 'The vague but powerful abstraction'.
12 To use Arcioni's felicitous phrase. E Arcioni 'The vague but powerful abstraction'. See *Roach v Electoral Commissioner* (2007) 239 ALR 1 at [8] per Gleeson CJ, [62] per Gummow, Kirby and Crennan JJ.
13 Mayo, 'The Theory of Democracy Outlined', p. 62.
14 J McMillan (2003) 'Constitutional reform – or constitutional delusion?', *Public Law Review*, vol. 14, p. 5.
15 J Kane 'Republicanism (Theory)' in *The Oxford Companion to Australian Politics*, (eds) B Galligan & W Roberts (2007), Oxford University Press, pp. 516–18.

Chapter 1

1   J Quick & R Garran (2000) *The Annotated Constitution of the Australian Commonwealth*, Law Books, p. 313.
2   Rather, colonial leaders stressed its other meanings. In 1891, Edmund Barton, who became Australia's first Prime Minister, traced its older meanings from the sixteenth and seventeenth century, quoting Shakespeare, Hobbes and Milton. Initially, the term was used to describe a government of any political persuasion – monarchy or democracy. With the end of the protectorate and the restoration of the monarchy, not surprisingly, the word 'gradually disappeared' from popular and political writing. (E Barton [1891] *The Draft Bill to Constitute the Commonwealth of Australia as adopted by the Convention of 1981*, Sydney Government Printer, pp. 9–11.) By 1891, it was a term used to describe the Federal Commonwealth of the United States and used to describe the British Commonwealth.
3   Quick & Garran, *Annotated Constitution*, p. 131.
4   Quick & Garran, *Annotated Constitution*, p. 311; *Official Record of the Debates of the Australasian Federal Convention, Sydney 1891* (1891), pp. 550–5.
5   Quick and Garran, *Annotated Constitution*, p. 131.
6   Quick and Garran, *Annotated Constitution*, p. 312.
7   Quick and Garran, *Annotated Constitution*, p. 368.

8. WJ Hudson & MP Sharp (1988) *Australian Independence: Colony to reluctant kingdom*, Melbourne University Press, p. 126.
9. J Warden (1993) 'The Fettered Republic: The Anglo-American Commonwealth and the Traditions of Australian Political Thought', *Australian Journal of Political Science*, vol. 28, pp. 83, 91.
10. Warden, 'The Fettered Republic', p. 91.
11. Warden, 'The Fettered Republic', p. 91.
12. W Hudson & M McKenna (2003) *Australian Republicanism: A Reader*, Melbourne University Press, p. 13.
13. Editorial (1806) 'Sydney', *Sydney Gazette*, 30 March; Warden, 'The Fettered Republic', p. 83.
14. V Vickers (2006) 'My Pen and Soul Have Gone Together' in *Thomas Paine and the American Revolution*, Routledge, p. 2.
15. Editorial (1842) 'The Australian', *The Australian*, 22 February; Vickers, 'My Pen and Soul', p. 2.
16. Hudson & McKenna, *Australian Republicanism*, p. 13.
17. Editorial, 'The Australian'.
18. Warden, 'The Fettered Republic', p. 91.
19. K Amos (1988) *The Fenians in Australia 1865–1880*, New South Wales University Press, chapter 3.
20. Warden, 'The Fettered Republic', p. 92.
21. Warden, 'The Fettered Republic', p. 92.
22. Warden, 'The Fettered Republic', p. 92.
23. Warden, 'The Fettered Republic', p. 83.
24. SM Herald (1887) 'The Riotous Meeting in Sydney', *Brisbane Courier*, 15 June.
25. Hudson & McKenna, *Australian Republicanism*, p. 75.
26. W Hudson & M McKenna (2007) 'Republicanism (history)', in *The Oxford Companion to Australian Politics*, (eds) B Galligan & W Roberts, Oxford University Press, pp. 514–16, 515.
27. Hudson & McKenna, 'Republicanism (history)', p. 515.
28. Hudson & McKenna, 'Republicanism (history)', p. 516.
29. S Macintyre (2004) *A Concise History of Australia*, Cambridge University Press, pp. 132–3.
30. F Alexander (1980) *Australia since Federation: A Narrative and Critical Analysis*, Nelson, p. 13.
31. Warden, 'The Fettered Republic', p. 90.
32. *Convention Debates* 1891, p. 185; Hudson & McKenna, *Australian Republicanism*, p. 113.
33. *Convention Debates* 1891, p. 186.
34. *Convention Debates* 1891, p. 185.
35. Warden, 'The Fettered Republic', p. 99.
36. Hudson & McKenna, *Australian Republicanism*, p. 113.
37. J La Nauze (1965) *Alfred Deakin: A Biography*, Melbourne University Press, pp. 475–6; see also Hudson & McKenna, *Australian Republicanism*, p. 141.
38. *Convention Debates* 1891, p.68.
39. Hudson & McKenna, 'Republicanism (history)', p. 516.
40. Hudson & Sharp, *Australian Independence*, pp. 49–56.
41. Hudson & McKenna, 'Republicanism (history)', pp. 6, 516.
42. M McKenna (1996) *A Captive Republic*, Press Syndicate of the University of Cambridge, p.10.

43 *Statute of Westminster Adoption Act 1942 (Cth)*, s 2; Hudson & Sharp, *Australian independence*, pp. 125, 136
44 D Lee (2004) 'Australia and the British Empire between the Wars', The Trevor Reese Memorial Lecture, London, King's College, p. 1; Goldsworthy, David (2002) *Losing the Blanket: Australia and the End of the British Empire*, Melbourne University Press, pp. 16–18.
45 AW Martin (1999) *Robert Menzies: A Life*, Melbourne University Press, pp. 454–5.
46 B Dyster & D Meredith (1990) *Australia in the International Economy in the Twentieth Century*, Cambridge University Press, pp. 248–52; JON Perkins 'Changing Economic Relations' in *Australia and Britain: Studies in a Changing Relationship*, (eds) AF Madden & WH Morris-Jones (1980), Sydney University Press in association with Institute of Commonwealth Studies, University of London, pp. 181–2.
47 Dyster & Meredith, *Australia in the International Economy*, p. 250.
48 S Ward (2001) *Australia and the British Embrace: The Demise of the Imperial Ideal*, Melbourne University Press, p. 253; Perkins, 'Changing Economic Relations', pp. 180, 182.
49 Hudson & McKenna, 'Republicanism (history)', p. 516.
50 *Sue v Hill* (1999) 199 CLR 462, 492.
51 McKenna, *A Captive Republic*, p. 5.
52 McKenna, *A Captive Republic*, p. 5.

Chapter 2

1 P Keating (1993) 'Advancing Australia: Building on Strength – the 1993 Federal Election' (Speech delivered at Bankstown, 24 February).
2 D Watson (2002) *Recollections of a Bleeding Heart: A Portrait of Paul Keating*, Random House Australia, p. 314.
3 C Bean (1993) 'Public Attitudes on the Monarchy–Republic Issue', *Australian Journal of Political Science*, vol. 28, pp. 191–6; R Morgan (1993) 'The Monarchy, the Media and the polls', <www.roymorgan.com/papers/1993/1993OC1.html>; S Poll (1992) *The Age*, 29 February; Newspoll (2005) 'Political & Issues Trends; Republic; In Favour or Against', <www.newspoll.com.au/cgi-bin/display_poll_data.pl>.
4 Bean, 'Public attitudes', p. 191; C Bean (2002) 'Political Personalities and Voting in the 1999 Australian Constitutional Referendum', *International Journal of Public Opinion Research*, vol. 14, p. 459; C Leithner (1994) 'Popular Support for "Mr Keating's Republic"', *Australian Journal of Political Science*, vol. 29, p. 354; B Tranter (1999) 'Public Support for an Australian Head of State' in *Proceedings of the 1999 Conference of the Australasian Political Studies Association*, (ed.) J Brookfield, Department of Government, University of Sydney, vol. 3.
5 Republic Advisory Committee (1993) *An Australian Republic: The Options*, AGPS, vol. 1.
6 Paul Keating (Telephone interview, 18 December 2008).
7 Watson, *Recollections of a Bleeding Heart*, p. 588.
8 Watson, *Recollections of a Bleeding Heart*, p. 202.
9 P Keating (1996) 'Australian Labor Party Policy Speech – 1996 Federal Election' (Speech delivered at ALP Campaign Launch, Melbourne, 14 February).

10 Keating had indicated his intention to put his vision of an Australian republic to the people in a referendum to be held 'some time in 1998 or 1999', and, if accepted, for the change to be implemented in 2001 on the centenary of Federation. (Commonwealth, Parliamentary Debates, House of Representatives, 7 June 1995, p. 1435 [Paul Keating, Prime Minister].)
11 Former Opposition Leader Alexander Downer had in fact proposed a referendum if agreement could be reached amongst republicans, the approach John Howard adopted when he became party leader in 1995. W Errington & P Van Onselen (2007) *John Winston Howard: The Definitive Biography*, Melbourne University Press, p. 218; John Howard (Telephone interview, 11 December 2008).
12 Watson, *Recollections of a Bleeding Heart*, pp. 588–9.
13 Watson, *Recollections of a Bleeding Heart*, p. 588.
14 Report of the Constitutional Convention (1998), AGPS.
15 Australian Electoral Commission (1997) 'Elected delegates' in *Constitutional Convention Election Report and Statistics*, p. 33, <http://www.aec.gov.au>; *Constitutional Convention (Election) Act 1997* (Cth).
16 Women's Constitutional Convention, 29–30 January 1998, *Outcomes*, <catalogue.nla.gov.au/Record/315171>.
17 Errington & Van Onselen, *John Winston Howard*, p. 285.
18 K Jones (2000) *The People's Protest*, ACM Publishing, p. 87.
19 For example, the McGarvie model, which advocated the least change to the Constitution, was supported by 32 delegates, 30 of whom were appointed (G Williams [1998] 'The 1998 Constitutional Conventions – first impressions', *Current Issues Brief,* 11, 23 March, p. 5, <www.aph.gov.au/library/pubs/cib/1997–98/98cib11.htm>.
20 The Yes/No pamphlet was posted to all Australian citizens by the Australian Electoral Commission (AEC). It contained the arguments for and against the proposed changes, as authorised by members of the Commonwealth Parliament who either favoured or opposed the changes. Australian Electoral Commission (1999) *Yes/No Pamphlet*, <www.australianpolitics.com/issues/republic/>.
21 Following the 1998 Convention, the following legislation was passed in both Houses of Parliament to implement the proposed 'Bipartisan appointment of the president model', *Constitution Alteration (Establishment of Republic) Act 1999* (Cth) and *Presidential Nominations Committee Act 1999* (Cth).
22 T Blackshield & G Williams (4th edn, 2006) *Australian Constitutional Law and Theory: Commentary and Materials*, Federation Press, p. 1452.
23 Errington & Van Onselen, *John Winston Howard*, p. 287.
24 John Howard (Telephone interview, 11 December 2008).
25 Prime Minister Howard's lack of interest in Australia's becoming a republic was demonstrated by the absence of any reference to the republic issue on his website or on the website of the Australian Liberal Party.
26 For more details see <www.chilli.net.au/~mcgarvie/paper45.htm>.
27 For more details of the report see chapter 4.
28 See <www.australia2020.gov.au/response/index.cfm>.
29 KA Walsh (2009) 'Talk is cheap on republic', *Sun Herald*, 26 April.
30 See <www.australia2020.gov.au/response/index.cfm>.
31 See <www.australia2020.gov.au/response/index.cfm>.

32 L Silmalis (2006) 'Republic back on the table', *Sunday Telegraph*, 14 June, p. 39; M Frankin (2009) 'All-round First', *The Australian* 30 March, p. 2.
33 R Morgan (2008) 'Now Only 45% of Australians Want a Republic with an Elected President (down 6% since 2001)', <www.roymorgan.com/news/polls/2008/4290/>.
34 Nielsen (2008) 'Majority favour a republic', *Federal Poll Report*, 21 September. Available upon request at <http://au.nielsen.com/site/index.shtml >.
35 Essential Research (2009) *Essential Report*, 2 February, p. 4.

Chapter 3

1 W Doyle (2001) *The French Revolution: A Very Short Introduction*, Oxford University Press, pp. 1–18.
2 PS Boyer (ed.) (2001) *The Oxford Companion to United States History*, Oxford University Press, pp. 664–6.
3 Notable exceptions are: J McMillan (2003) 'Constitutional reform – or constitutional delusion?' *Public Law Review*, vol. 14, p. 5; and G Williams (2006) 'Why Australia Kept the Queen', *Saskatchewan Law Review*, vol. 63, p. 477. Some constitutional lawyers have dealt with, inter alia, the procedural requirements of section 128. See for example: Patrick Keyzer (2nd edn, 2005) *Constitutional Law*, LexisNexis Australia, pp. 24–5; P Hanks, P Keyzer & J Clarke (7th edn, 2004) *Australian Constitutional Law*, LexisNexis Butterworths, pp. 47–9; P Hanks (2nd edn, 1996) *Constitutional Law in Australia*, Butterworths, pp. 28–30; B Harris & D Barker (eds) (2nd edn, 2004) *Essential Constitutional Law*, Cavendish Publishing Pty Limited, pp. 21–2. In addition, constitutional lawyers have examined the relationship of section 128 to different modes of constitutional interpretation. A Twomey (2008) 'Constitutional Alteration and the High Court', *University of Queensland Law Journal*, vol. 21(1), pp. 47–69.
T Blackshield & G Williams (4th edn, 2006) *Australian Constitutional Law and Theory*, Federation Press, pp. 1382–7.
4 McMillan, 'Constitutional reform – or constitutional delusion?', p. 5.
5 McMillan, 'Constitutional reform – or constitutional delusion?', p. 5.
6 Section 128 of the Australian Constitution is the only section which specifies various procedures for constitutional amendment.
7 This requirement in section 128 is to provide 'sufficient time for the electors to inform themselves of the issue and to prevent undue delay'. MW Harrison (1997) *The Constitution of the Commonwealth of Australia*, Legal Books, St Leonards, p. 600.
8 Australian Constitution s 128.
9 The procedure under s 128 covers various forms of disagreement between the Houses. However, the following procedure must be followed: the Senate must have failed to pass the Bill or rejected it, or passed the proposal in amended form to which the House of Representatives will not agree. If the House persists, after a period of three months has elapsed it must pass the proposal a second time with an absolute majority. Then the Bill can be put to the people, irrespective of the attitude of the Senate at the time.

10 See Harrison, *The Constitution of the Commonwealth of Australia*, p. 591; RM Dworkin (1977) 'Is law a system of rules?' in *The Philosophy of Law*, (ed.) RM Dworkin, Oxford University Press.
11 Under the Australian Constitution, the Governor-General has a discretion to put the Bill to a referendum, because s 128 uses the word 'may', which is directory and not mandatory. According to the doctrine of responsible government, this discretion will only be exercised on the advice of the Prime Minister.
12 Harrison, *The Constitution of the Commonwealth of* Australia, p. 600.
13 Harrison, *The Constitution of the Commonwealth of Australia*, p. 600.
14 McMillan, 'Constitutional reform – or constitutional delusion?', p. 5.
15 See also RD Lumb (1989) 'The bi-centenary of Australian constitutionalism', *University of Queensland Law Journal*, vol. 15, pp. 3–32; S Ratnapala (2nd edn, 2007) 'Basic norm of the Constitution' in *Australian Constitutional Law: Foundations and theory*, Oxford University Press, p. 325; Blackshield & Williams, *Australian Constitutional Law and Theory*, pp. 1382–7.
16 Paul Keating (Telephone interview, 18 December 2008).
17 Keating, 18 December 2008.
18 Keating, 18 December 2008.
19 M Turnbull (1999) *Fighting for the Republic*, Hardie Grant Books, p. 2.
20 Keating, 18 December 2008.
21 Keating, 18 December 2008.
22 Prime Minister Paul Keating (1995), 'An Australian Republic: The Way Forward' (Speech delivered at the House of Representatives, Canberra, 7 June).
23 Keating, 18 December 2008.
24 Keating, 18 December 2008.
25 John Howard (Telephone interview, 11 December 2008).
26 Howard, 11 December 2008.
27 Howard, 11 December 2008.
28 Howard, 11 December 2008.
29 Legal and Constitutional References Committee, Senate (2004), *The Road to a Republic*, August.
30 G Michael (2001) 'Labor's fast-track republic', *The Age*, 21 July.
31 C Uhlmann (2008) 'Rudd talks regulation and republic', ABC Radio, *AM*, 21 April.
32 M Grattan (2008) 'The Turnbull ascendancy – Liberal Leadership', *The Age*, 17 September.
33 Grattan, 'The Turnbull ascendancy'.
34 J Warhurst (2008) 'Bipartisan backing for a republic can be achieved', *The Canberra Times*, 25 September, p. 19.
35 Keating, 18 December 2008.
36 P Keating (2000) *Engagement: Australia faces the Asia-Pacific*, Macmillan, pp. 266–7.
37 For example, the bipartisan composition of the committee was: chaired by Malcolm Turnbull, included prominent Liberal Party members (Nick Greiner and Naomi Dougal) and constitutional experts (Professor Winterton and Dr John Hirst).
38 Howard, 11 December 2008.
39 Howard, 11 December 2008.
40 Commonwealth, Parliamentary Debates, House of Representatives,

8 June 1995, p. 1620 (John Howard, Leader of the Opposition).
41 Howard, 11 December 2008.
42 Howard, 11 December 2008.
43 Turnbull, *Fighting for the Republic*, pp. 1, 22–3.
44 This stage one plebiscite would ask whether Australia should become a republic with an Australian head of state, separating from the British monarchy. The purpose of this plebiscite would be to legitimise support for an Australian republic and to justify expenditure on the following three stages. The chances of success of such a plebiscite in Australia are quite good. Majority support for a republic exists in Australia.
45 According to stage two, if Australians vote 'Yes' in the first plebiscite, they would be given an opportunity to vote in a second plebiscite indicating five alternative methods for appointing the head of state. The committee also recommended that this second plebiscite contain other relevant questions, such as the preferred title for an Australian head of state. The first plebiscite (Stage 1) would be based on a simple majority and the second plebiscite (Stage 2) would be conducted on a preferential voting basis. Voting in both plebiscites would be compulsory, as is the practice in Australia for all elections. The apparent purpose of the proposal is to give everyone a chance to have their say and to express their preferences about the type of republic Australia should become.
46 The purpose of the drafting convention is to finetune the details of the preferred type of republic, based on the result of the second plebiscite, and to prepare drafting instructions for an amendment to the Constitution. The committee recommended that membership of the convention should be comprised of constitutional experts and others with recognised relevant skills and abilities, and that it should reflect Australia's gender, ethnic and age diversity. Members of the convention would be appointed by both Houses of Parliament after consultation with the parliamentary political parties. One of the consequences of the convention is that it would be likely to ensure that the model is workable and credible. The process would also mollify concerns over the dangers associated with the proposed model.
47 Legal and Constitutional References Committee, August 2004. Stage 4 would involve the Bills being passed through the Federal Parliament and a referendum being put to the Australian people in accordance with the procedure set down in s 128 of the Australian Constitution, supra note 19. While the first three stages would be non-binding, it is a constitutional requirement that the last referendum be legally binding. This final step would also assure the people that they will have the final say.
48 See the *Plebiscite for an Australian Republic Bill 2008* (Cth).
49 These points were raised in a forum where speeches were given by Shadow Attorney-General Nicola Roxon and Liberal Senator Mitch Fifield at the Australian Republican Movement. N Roxon & M Fifield (2005) 'The Republic: Which Way Forward?' (Speech to the Australian Republican Movement, Melbourne, 22 November).
50 Commonwealth, Senate Legal and Constitutional References Committee, 18 May 2004, 1 (Professor Greg Craven).

51 This special majority would require bipartisan support and thus ensure that the head of state would be blessed by all major parties. Such a vote would also encourage cooperation.
52 The Keating Government rejected a comprehensive code of the head of state's powers because it could not be written 'in a way that would both find general community acceptance and cover every possible contingency'.
53 The Keating Government contended that the good sense of the people will ensure an appropriate outcome for Australia. Under the constitutional amending procedure, a majority of people in four States would be required to introduce a Commonwealth republic. Consequently, two States may realistically remain monarchies after a successful referendum.
54 Constitutional Convention Resolutions passed on 12 February (1998), Department of Prime Minister and Cabinet, viewed 20 April 1998, <http://www.dpmc.gov.au/convention/speak_note/resols9.html>.
55 See Australian Constitution s 44.
56 Legal and Constitutional Committee, August 2004.
57 Committee Hansard, 13 April 2004, p. 45.
58 *Referendum (Machinery Provisions) Act 1984* (Cth) s 25, schedule 1, form B.
59 Joint Select Committee on the Republic Referendum, Commonwealth Parliament, Advisory Report of the Joint Select Committee (Establishment of Republic) 1999 and Constitution Alteration (Establishment of Republic), August 1999, p. 9.
60 Joint Select Committee on the Republic Referendum, Advisory Report, p. 12.
61 Howard, 11 December 2008.
62 Kim Beazley (Telephone interview, 11 December 2008).
63 The decision was unanimous of all members present voting on the report. Bob Charles notes: '... we had a unanimous outcome on the day and that was true. Now, you don't get unanimous outcomes if people haven't had an opportunity to have their say and if they're not satisfied that they've reached the best compromise of their views with others' views to get a reliable outcome'. (Bob Charles, Telephone interview, 4 February 2009.)
64 Joint Select Committee on the Republic Referendum, Commonwealth Parliament, p. 12.
65 Charles, 4 February 2009.
66 Beazley, 11 December 2008.
67 Howard, 11 December 2008.
68 Howard, 11 December 2008.
69 Howard, 11 December 2008.
70 Howard, 11 December 2008.
71 Charles, 4 February 2009.
72 Beazley, 11 December 2008.
73 'Referendum Question', Transcript of *7:30 Report*, 9 August 1999, <www.abc.net.au/7.30/stories/s42572.htm>.
74 T Wright (1999) 'PM's New Republic Blow', *The Age*, 9 August, p. 1.
75 Howard, 11 December 2008.
76 Beazley, 11 December 2008.

77 'Referendum Question', Transcript of *7:30 Report.*
78 Charles, 4 February 2009.
79 *Referendum (Machinery Provisions) Act 1984* (Cth) s. 11.
80 Commonwealth, Parliamentary Debates, House of Representatives, 16 December 1912, p. 7154 (Hughes, Attorney-General).
81 Commonwealth, Parliamentary Debates, House of Representatives, 16 December 1912, p. 7156 (Fischer, Prime Minister and Treasurer). See also D Freeman (1999) 'Public Information Machinery and the 1999 Referenda, *Public Law Review*, vol. 10, p. 243.
82 C Saunders (1984) 'Referendum Procedures', Report to Standing Committee, Australian Constitutional Convention Constitutional Amendment Sub-Committee, pp. 113–14. See also Freeman, 'Public Information Machinery', p. 243.
83 Saunders 'Referendum Procedures', pp. 111, 113–14. See also Freeman, 'Public Information Machinery', p. 243.
84 *Referendum (Machinery Provisions) Act 1984* (Cth) s 11(4).
85 *Referendum Legislation Amendment Act 1999* (Cth) No. 22 s 4.
86 Freeman, 'Public Information Machinery', pp. 224–5; Commonwealth, Parliamentary Debates, House of Representatives, 11 March 1999, p. 3762 (Williams, Attorney-General).
87 Freeman, 'Public Information Machinery', p. 225.
88 Freeman, 'Public Information Machinery', p. 223.
89 Commonwealth, Parliamentary Debates, House of Representatives, 11 March 1999, p. 3761 (Williams, Attorney-General).
90 Commonwealth, Parliamentary Debates, House of Representatives, 11 March 1999, pp. 3761–2 (Williams, Attorney-General).
91 Freeman, 'Public Information Machinery', p. 223; *Referendum (Machinery Provisions) Act 1984* (Cth) s 11(1) (2); *Referendum Legislation Amendment Act 1999* (Cth) No. 22 s 4.
92 K Beazley (2000) 'Planning for a New Republic' (Speech delivered to the Australian Association for Constitutional Law, Notre Dame University, Fremantle, 7 October).
93 Freeman, 'Public Information Machinery', p. 247.

Chapter 4

1 W Bagehot (2nd edn, 1978) *The English Constitution*, Garland Publishing, p.33.
2 Bagehot, *The English Constitution*, p. 37.
3 Bagehot, *The English Constitution*, p. 37.
4 George Washington was elected the first President of the United States in February 1789. See (ed.) PS Boyer (2001) *The Oxford Companion to United States History*, Oxford University Press, pp.156–8.
5 DJ Gow, C Bean & I McAllister (2000) *Australian Constitutional Referendum Study, 1999: User's Guide for the Machine-Readable Data File*, Social Science Data Archives; Social Research Centre (2008) *Public Opinion Towards Governance: Results from the Inaugural ANU Poll*, Australian National University, April, p. 8.
6 For a general discussion of the principles of responsible government see H Emy & O Hughes (1991) *Australian Politics: Realities in Conflict*, Macmillan, p. 336 ff.
7 D Smith (2005) 'The dismissal: Setting the record straight' in *Head of*

    State: The Governor-General, the Monarchy, the Republic and the Dismissal, Macleay Press, pp. 89–90.
8 *The King v The Governor of the State of South Australia* (1907) 4 CLR 1497, 1511 per Griffith CJ, Barton, O'Connor, Isaacs and Higgins JJ.
9 PH Lane (1986) *Lane's Commentary on the Australian Constitution*, Law Book Company, p. 17.
10 Constitutional Commission, Commonwealth Government, *Final Report of the Constitutional Commission* (1988), p. 313.
11 Constitutional Commission, *Final Report*, p. 311.
12 P Hanks, P Keyzer & J Clarke (7th edn, 2004) *Australian Constitutional Law: Materials and Commentary*, Butterworths, p. 465.
13 *Royal Powers Act 1953* (Cth) s 2(1): 'At any time when the Queen is personally present in Australia, any power under an Act exercisable by the Governor-General may be exercised by the Queen.' In 1953 both the Senate and the House of Representatives amended their standing orders to provide that, when the Queen is present in Australia, references to the Governor-General should be read as references to the Queen (Smith, *Head of State*, p. 97). See for example: C Harris (ed.) (5th edn, 2005) *House of Representatives Practice*, Department of the House of Representatives, p. 225.
14 However, some functions of an English monarch may not be as applicable to an Australian Governor-General. In the quaint and rather mysterious words of Walter Bagehot: 'The occupations of a constitutional monarch are grave, formal, important, but never exciting; they have nothing to stir eager blood, awaken high imagination, work off wild thoughts', (Bagehot, *The English Constitution*, p. 53).
15 While the Governor-General is not a member of a political party, it should be noted that a number of Governors-General had previously served as politicians. For example, Isaac Isaacs served, amongst other things, as the federal Attorney-General under Sir Alfred Deakin's government, and prior to his appointment as Australia's 21st Governor-General, Bill Hayden was a former Opposition Leader and a member of the ALP who had served as a Minister in the Whitlam Government.
16 Legal and Constitutional References Committee, Senate (2004), *The Road to a Republic*, August, p. 55.
17 Legal and Constitutional References Committee, *The Road to a Republic*, p. 55.
18 B Doherty (2008) 'G-G fears towns will succumb to twin perils of economy and drought', *The Age*, 25 October, p. 5.
19 M Grattan (2009) 'New G-G strides in a wide world', *The Age*, 6 March, p. 15; A Bolt (2009) 'Generally speaking Ms Bryce you are out of your territory', *Herald Sun*, 6 March, p. 40.
20 P Hasluck (1979) *The Office of Governor-General*, Melbourne University Press, p. 23.
21 Lane, *Lane's Commentary on the Australian Constitution*, p. 21.
22 Lane, *Lane's Commentary on the Australian Constitution*, p. 21.
23 Harris, *House of Representatives Practice*, pp. 214–20.
24 Alternatively, it closes because of the expiry of the three-year term of the House of Representatives.
25 'To prorogue Parliament means to bring to an end a session of

Parliament without dissolving the House of Representatives or both Houses, and, therefore, without a subsequent election. Prorogation has the effect of terminating all business pending before the Houses and Parliament does not meet again until the date specified in the proroguing proclamation or until the Houses are summoned to meet again by the Governor-General': H Evans (ed.) (12th edn, 2008) *Odges*, Commonwealth of Australia, pp. 141–2; Harris, *House of Representatives Practice*, pp. 225–6; May in Lane, *Lane's Commentary on the Australian Constitution*, p. 22: 'Every bill must therefore be renewed after a prorogation, as if it had never been introduced.'

26 Lane, *Lane's Commentary on the Australian Constitution*, p. 21.
27 Smith, *Head of State*, p. 253.
28 Office of the Governor-General of the Commonwealth of Australia 'Governor-General's Role' (2008), viewed 8 May 2009, <www.gg.gov.au/governorgeneral/category.php?id=2>.
29 <www.gg.ca/gg/rr/index_e.asp>.
30 An Inter-State Commission, 'with ... powers of adjudication and administration ... relating to trade and commerce', was established by section 101 of the Australian Constitution. This body no longer exists.
31 This term means that an issue is not capable of being settled by a court of law.
32 Breach of these rules may have real consequences for political actors, the Crown, the Ministers and the Parliament, who have responsibility for administering them. Hanks et al, *Australian Constitutional Law*, p. 493. Responsible government is a convention of the constitution that in general requires that the powers of the Governor-General are exercised upon the advice of the Prime Minister and/or Ministers. Hanks et al, *Australian Constitutional Law*, pp. 492–3.
33 J Quick & R Garran (1901) *The Annotated Constitution of the Australian Commonwealth*, Legal Books, p. 406. See also *Western Australia v Commonwealth (the Territorial Senators case)* (1975) 134 CLR 201, 278 per Jacobs J.
34 Bagehot, *The English Constitution*, p. 75.
35 Republican Advisory Committee (1993) *An Australian Republic: The Options – the Report*, Australian Government Publishing Service, p. 26.
36 G Winterton (1993) 'Presidential Power in Republican Australia', *Australian Journal of Political Science*, vol. 28, p. 42.
37 Republican Advisory Committee, *An Australian Republic*, p. 35.
38 Republican Advisory Committee, *An Australian Republic*, p. 24.
39 Republican Advisory Committee, *An Australian Republic*, p. 24
40 *Minister for Arts, Heritage and Environment v Peko Wallsend Ltd* (1987) 75 ALR 218, 225 per Bowen CJ. See also Hanks et al, *Australian Constitutional Law*, p. 490
41 Anderson 'The Constitutional Framework' in *The Government of the Australian States*, (ed.) RS Davis (1960), Longmans, p. 11.
42 Hanks et al, *Australian Constitutional Law*, p. 490.
43 Legal power is not vested in the Cabinet by the Constitution or legislation (Bowen CJ in *Minister for Arts, Heritage and Environment v Peko Wallsend Ltd* [1987] 75 ALR 218, 222).
44 Although the Constitution makes reference to the Queen's Ministers of State, who must also become Members of Parliament within three

months of their appointment (Australian Constitution s 64).
45. Sawer (1956) 'Cabinets, Councils and Ministers in Australia', *Public Law*, pp. 110, 116.
46. Sawer, 'Cabinets Councils and Ministers in Australia', p. 116.
47. Republic Advisory Committee, *An Australian Republic: The Options – the Report*, p. 36. Sawer, 'Cabinets, Councils and Ministers', p. 116. These decisions include the power to make regulations or subordinate laws, which are authorised by a statute. For instance, the government will pass an act through Parliament authorising the Governor-General in Council to make regulations which spell out in more detail how the Act is to operate in practice. The power to make subordinate laws is a very significant power. The justification for dividing legal and political power in this way is efficiency. It was thought that Cabinet discussion ought not be bogged down by the need to succinctly make a decision capable of recognition in the law. However, today this rational is not once as strong as it was, with Cabinet Secretaries taking careful notes.
48. Australian Constitution s 5.
49. Australian Constitution s 57.
50. Australian Constitution s 64.
51. Australian Constitution s 53.
52. Hanks et al, *Australian Constitutional Law*, pp. 498–9.
53. M Sexton (1979) *Illusions of Power: The Fate of a Reform Government*, George Allen & Unwin Australia Pty Ltd, p.128; 'This tactic accounted for the defeat of 93 Bills in the government's 35 months of office. In the previous 75 years of the Senate's history, it had rejected outright a total of only 68 Bills.'
54. M Coper & W George (eds) (1997) *Power, Parliament and the People*, Federation Press, p. 186.
55. Commonwealth, Parliamentary Debates, Senate 5 April 1973, p. 915.
56. Commonwealth, Parliamentary Debates, Senate 5 April 1973, p. 915.
57. Sexton, *Illusions of Power*, p. 125.
58. Hanks et al, *Australian Constitutional Law*, p. 499.
59. G Winterton (2003) '1975: The Dismissal of the Whitlam Government' in *Australian Constitutional Landmarks*, (eds) HP Lee & G Williams, Federation Press, pp. 229, 242.
60. Hanks et al, *Australian Constitutional Law*, p. 499.
61. Hanks et al, *Australian Constitutional Law*, p. 499.
62. Smith, *Head of State*, p. 258.
63. Smith, *Head of State*, p. 258.
64. G Whitlam, 'Reflections on 1975: The coup 20 years after' in *Power, Parliament and the People*, Coper & Williams, p. 138.
65. Whitlam, 'Reflections on 1975', p. 145.
66. Editorial (1995) 'Unresolved: the class of power', *The Weekend Australian*, 11–12 November, p. 22.
67. Hanks et al, *Australian Constitutional Law*, p. 505.
68. Hanks et al, *Australian Constitutional Law*, pp. 499–501.
69. Hanks et al, *Australian Constitutional Law*, p. 499.
70. See Hanks et al, *Australian Constitutional Law*, p. 503.
71. Sawer in Hanks et al, *Australian Constitutional Law*, p. 507.
72. Winterton, '1975: The Dismissal of the Whitlam Government', p. 252.

73 *Parliament Act 1911* (UK).
74 Republican Advisory Committee, *An Australian Republic*, p. 31.
75 Hanks et al, *Australian Constitutional Law*, p. 498.
76 Hanks et al, *Australian Constitutional Law*, p. 498.
77 Winterton, '1975: The Dismissal of the Whitlam Government', pp. 245, 247.
78 South Australia (1897) *Official Report of the National Australian Convention Debates*, Adelaide, 22 March – 5 May, p. 908 (George Reid).
79 South Australia, Convention Debates, p. 910 (Edmond Barton); Quick & Garran, *The Annotated Constitution of the Australian Commonwealth*, p. 707.
80 AJ Ward 'Australia and Parliamentary Orthodoxy: A Foreign Perspective on Australian Constitutional Reform' in *Australia and Parliamentary Orthodoxy: A Foreign Perspective on Australian Constitutional Reform* (Papers on Parliament No. 35, June 2000), p. 63.
81 Ward, 'Australia and Parliamentary Orthodoxy', p. 63.

Chapter 5

1 P Keating (1995) 'An Australian Republic: The Way Forward', (Speech delivered at Parliament House, Canberra, 7 June).
2 Keating, 'An Australian Republic: The Way Forward'.
3 Keating, 'An Australian Republic: The Way Forward'.
4 Australian Electoral Commission (1999) *Yes/No Referendum 99: Your official Referendum pamphlet*, pp. 8, 10.
5 Australian Constitution s 2.
6 J Kerr (1978) *Matters for Judgement*, Sun Books, p. 329.
7 See G Winterton (1995) 'The States and the Republic: A Constitutional Accord?', *Public Law Review*, vol. 6, p. 107.
8 *Constitution Alteration (Establishment of Republic) 1999 Bill* (Cth) s 60. I have abbreviated the process to highlight the introduction of democratic authority.
9 See, for example, *Lange v Australian Broadcasting Corporation* (1997) 189 CLR 520; *Coleman v Power* (2004) 220 CLR 1.
10 A Stone (2005) 'Text and Structure Revisited', *University of New South Wales Law Journal*, vol. 23(3), pp. 842, 844.
11 A Stone (1999) 'The Limits of Constitutional Text and Structure: Standards of Review and the Freedom of Political Communication', *Melbourne University Law Review*, vol. 23, pp. 668, 686; Cf. *Coleman v Power* (2004) 220 CLR 1, pp. 48–53 per J McHugh.
12 The simple words 'directly chosen by the people' have given rise to the implication in the Australian Constitution of representative government which establishes a freedom of political communication. See *Lange v Australian Broadcasting Corporation* (1997) 189 CLR 520; *Coleman v Power*.
13 *A–G (Commonwealth); Ex rel McKinlay v Commonwealth* (1975) 135 CLR 1, 65 per J Murphy.
14 P Boyce (2007) 'Monarchy' in *The Oxford Companion to Australian Politics*, (eds) B Galligan & W Roberts, Oxford University Press, p. 347.

15   G Williams (1995) 'A Republican Tradition for Australia?', *Federal Law Review*, vol. 23, p. 133, 136; J Harrington 'The Commonwealth of Oceana' in *The Commonwealth of Oceana and a system of politics*, (ed.) PGA Pocock (1992), Cambridge University Press, pp. 8–42.
16   For another vision of republican self-government see Sunstein who extols four key principles: deliberation, political equality, universalism and citizenship. C Sustein (1988) 'Beyond the Republican Revival', *Yale Law Journal*, vol. 97, p. 1539.
17   A monarch is literally a sole ruler.
18   M McKenna (1996) *The Captive Republic*, Press Syndicate of the University of Cambridge, p. 8.
19   See R Dahl (1989) *Democracy and its Critics*, Yale University Press.
20   C Sunstein 'The Enduring Legacy of Republicanism' in *A New Constitutionalism,* (eds) S Elkin & K Soltan (1993), University of Chicago Press, p. 174, 175. See J Warden (1993) 'The Fettered Republic: The Anglo-American Commonwealth and the Traditions of Australian Thought', *Australian Journal of Political Science*, vol. 28, pp. 83, 88; C Sunstein (1985) 'Interest Groups in American Public Law', *Stanford Law Review*, vol. 38, pp. 29, 45. It is noteworthy that the wishes of some of the American Founders were that those who own the land should run the country. Hence the experience in the United States has been that private interests did affect the government: see Williams, 'A Republican tradition for Australia?', p. 136.
21   J Madison, *The Federalist*, no. 10, 23 November 1787 in *The Federalist Papers*, (ed.) Clinton Rossiter (1961), Penguin Books Ltd, p. 82. This understanding is surprisingly close to the Burkean conception of representation. See, for example, Speech to the Electors, 3 November 1774, reprinted in *Burke's Politics: Selected Writings and Speeches on Reform, Revolution and War*, (ed.) RJS Hoffman (1949) AA Knopf, p. 116. See also S Miller (1983) *Special Interest Groups in American Politics*, Transaction Books, pp. 52–3.
22   Dahl, *Democracy and its Critics*, p. 25.
23   For a contemporary commentary on related issues see: A Little (2007) 'Between disagreement and consensus: unravelling the democratic paradox', *Australian Journal of Political Science*, vol. 42(1), pp. 143–59; C Sunstein (2003) *Why Societies Need Dissent*, Harvard University Press.
24   P Pettit (1992) 'Republican Themes', *Legislative Studies*, vol. 6(2), pp. 29, 29.
25   P Pettit (1993) 'Liberalism and Republicanism', *Australian Journal of Political Science*, vol. 28, pp. 162, 176.
26   Pettit, 'Liberalism and Republicanism', p. 176.
27   Pettit, 'Liberalism and Republicanism', p. 176.
28   McKenna, *The Captive Republic*, p. 5.
29   Warden, 'The Fettered Republic', p. 92.
30   McKenna, *The Captive Republic*, p. 5.
31   McKenna, *The Captive Republic*, p. 5.
32   McKenna, *The Captive Republic*, p. 5.
33   McKenna, *The Captive Republic*, p. 4.
34   McKenna, *The Captive Republic*; Warden 'The Fettered Republic'.
35   M McKenna & W Hudson (eds) (2003) *Australian Republicanism: A Reader*, Melbourne University Press.

36 See I Honohan & J Jennings (2005) *Republicanism in Theory and Practice*, Routledge, pp. 8–12.
37 See, for example, Pettit, 'Liberalism and Republicanism'; A Fraser (1995) 'In Defence of Republicanism: A Reply to George Williams', *Federal Law Review*, vol. 23, p. 362; (eds) J Hoorn and D Goodman (1996) *Vox Republicae: Feminism and the Republic*, La Trobe University Press; McKenna, *The Captive Republic*, pp. 4–5. See also <www.womenrep.netspeed.com.au>.
38 Republic Advisory Committee, Parliament of Australia, *An Australian Republic: The Options – the Report* (1993), p. 39.
39 Republic Advisory Committee, *An Australian Republic*, p. 39.
40 Republic Advisory Committee, *An Australian Republic*, p. 39.
41 Republic Advisory Committee, *An Australian Republic*, p. 39.
42 A Fenna (2008) 'A Political Science Perspective', Paper presented at Planning for a Republic – The Legal Mechanic's Perspective, Perth, 29 November.
43 Fenna, 'A Political Science Perspective'.
44 Fenna, 'A Political Science Perspective'.
45 Here constitutional lawyers and political scientists may differ. Differing classifications depend upon the circumstances and thus Australia's system of government may be simultaneously classified as: a representative democracy; a federation; a responsible government; or a nation state.
46 P Hanks, P Keyzer & J Clarke (2004) *Australian Constitutional Law: Materials and Commentary*, Butterworths, p. 464.
47 Hanks et al, *Australian Constitutional Law*, p. 464.
48 Hanks et al, *Australian Constitutional Law*, p. 464 (references removed).
49 Hanks et al, *Australian Constitutional Law*, p. 464.
50 Hanks et al, *Australian Constitutional Law*, pp. 465–6. Today, the Queen's only formal power is to appoint and remove her representative.
51 B Galligan (1993) 'Regularizing the Australian Republic', *Australian Journal of Political Science*, vol. 28, Special Issue, p. 56.
52 B Galligan (1995) *A Federal Republic*, Cambridge University Press, p. 25.
53 Commentators have been questioning the efficacy of minimalism and rethinking the mechanics of constitutional amendment. Professor Cheryl Saunders recently reflected upon its future, explaining its attractions and detractions. On the one hand, minimalism's strengths are that it fits in well with Australia's gradual story of independence and constitutional culture. It also addresses the concern that '[a]mbitious change might destabilise aspects of our system of government such as responsible government, federalism [and] the rule of law'. Minimalism is also consistent with the belief that minor proposals have been thought more likely to succeed given the low success rate of constitutional referenda in Australia. On the other hand, it seems that minor constitutional amendments have actually been unsuccessful, as was the case in the 1999 republican referendum and the 1988 referendums. In many ways, minimalism obscures the implications of constitutional monarchy that could change in the shift to an Australian republic.

C Saunders (2008) 'Implementing Models', Paper presented at Planning for a Republic – The Legal Mechanic's Perspective, Perth, 29 November.
54 Saunders, 'Implementing Models'.
55 Paul Keating (Telephone interview, 18 December 2008).

Chapter 6

1. M Krygier 'Between Fear and Hope', Boyer Lectures, 16 November 1997, Lecture 2, viewed 11 March 2009, <www.abc.net.au/rn/boyerlectures/stories/1997/988491.htm>.
2. Krygier, 'Between Fear and Hope'.
3. G Winterton (2001) 'The Resurrection of the Republic' (Paper presented at Centre for International and Public Law, Faculty of Law, Australian National University, Canberra), Federation Press, p. 7.
4. Cabinet (2009) 'Prime Minister of Australia', viewed 27 February 2009, <www.pm.gov.au/team/cabinet.cfm>.
5. Parliament of Australian Senate (2009) *List of Senators*, viewed 6 March 2009, <http://www.aph.gov.au/Senate/senators/contacts/los.htm>.
6. <http://www.aec.gov.au/Enrolling_to_vote/Enrolment_stats/index.htm>.
7. Australian Constitution s 2. Up until the 1930s this advice was tendered by British Ministers. Today the Queen acts exclusively on the advice of her Australian Ministers.
8. Australian Constitution s 72.
9. *Presidential Nominations Committee Bill 1999* (Cth).
10. J Madison (1787) 'The Federalist', no. 10, 23 November, in *The Federalist Papers*, (ed.) C Rossiter (1961), Penguin Books Ltd, p. 82.
11. W Bagehot (2nd edn, 1978) *The English Constitution*, Garland Publishing, p. 45.
12. *Presidential Nominations Committee Bill 1999* (Cth) cl 22.
13. The Committee process has been criticised: The Prime Minister could ignore the Committee's nomination; the committee's deliberations would be in private and confidential. These criticisms have answers. It is not the function of the Committee to pick the candidate themselves, the choice rests with the elected representatives: the Prime Minister and the Parliament. The nominations and report would be secret, but this is in order to protect confidentiality. (*Presidential Nominations Committee Bill 1999* (Cth) cl 23, 24, 25.). The Nomination Committee process could have been improved. There is virtue in allowing the list of committee nominations and possibly the merits of each candidate to be made public with the consent of the candidates.
14. *Presidential Nominations Committee Bill 1999* (Cth) cl 22. The Presidential Nominations Committee would be composed of 32 members including: eight Commonwealth; eight State/Territory and; eight community. *Presidential Nominations Committee Bill 1999* (Cth) cl 8. The Prime Minister was to select community and Commonwealth representatives, and the States and Territories were to select their own representatives. *Presidential Nominations Committee Bill 1999* (Cth) cl 9–11.

The role of the committee was: to invite and consider nominations for appointment for the President to give the Prime Minister a report on the nominations. (*Presidential Nominations Committee Bill 1999* (Cth) cl 5.)

15 R Hunter 'Working the Republic: Some Feminist Reflections' in *Vox Reipublicae*, (eds) J Hoorn & D Goodman (1996), La Trobe University Press, p. 59.
16 Hunter, 'Working the Republic: Some Feminist Reflections', p. 59.
17 Hunter, 'Working the Republic: Some Feminist Reflections', p. 59.
18 Hunter, 'Working the Republic: Some Feminist Reflections', p. 59.
19 K Murphy (2009) 'G-G opts out of gun patronage', *The Age*, 26 February.
20 Winterton, 'The Resurrection of the Republic', p. 8.
21 Winterton, 'The Resurrection of the Republic', pp. 8–9. See, for example, WC Müller, 'Austria' in *Semi-Presidentialism in Europe*,(ed.) R Elgie (1999), Oxford Scholarship Online Monographs, 22, pp. 43–6.
22 Winterton, 'The Resurrection of the Republic', p. 10.
23 Winterton, 'The Resurrection of the Republic', p. 9.
24 AJ Ward, 'Australia and Parliamentary Orthodoxy: A Foreign Perspective on Australian Constitutional Reform' in *Australia and Parliamentary Orthodoxy: A Foreign Perspective on Australian Constitutional Reform* (Papers on Parliament No. 35, June 2000), 63, p. 76.
25 D Held (1987) *Models of Democracy*, Stanford University Press, p. 21.
26 Held, *Models of Democracy*, p. 63.
27 See also Winterton, 'The Resurrection of the Republic', p. 10.
28 *Electoral Act 1918* (Cth) s 93.
29 HD Mayo (1960) *An Introduction to Democracy*, Oxford University Press, p. 107.
30 The franchise is now prescribed by the Commonwealth *Electoral Act 1918* (Cth). In Australia, for a person to run for office, they must be qualified to vote and not be subject to any of the disqualifications, which include, persons who have mental incapacity, non citizens, non residents, some prisoners, persons who have committed treason and not been pardoned. See *Commonwealth Electoral Act 1918* (Cth) ss 93, 94. In addition to the disqualifications for voters, a candidate must avoid the additional disqualifications of candidates for the Federal Parliament in the Australian Constitution. These disqualifications, which were proposed to be applied in the referendum model, pertain to dual allegiances, treason, bankruptcy, employment as a paid government officer, and pecuniary interest in a contract with the Commonwealth Government (Australian Constitution s 44). Some of these disqualifications have been contentious. The disqualifications of holders of office of profit under the Crown have excluded persons employed by government departments such as a school teacher. See *Sykes v Cleary and Others (No 2)* (1992) 109 ALR 577. A person owing a foreign allegiance has excluded persons who have not renounced their dual nationality (catching British, Swiss and Greek citizens) (*Sykes v Cleary and Others (No 2)* and *Sue v Hill* (1999) 199 CLR 462.)

A head of state should not have a conflict of allegiance, nor should they hold an office of government other than President. However, the current Constitution discourages such people from standing for office since 'they are incapable of being chosen' (Australian Constitution s 44). This means a public servant must resign, and a foreign citizen must renounce their citizenship prior to the day they nominate for office. These disincentives could be removed if the Constitution permitted resignation or renunciation after the results of the poll are published on election night, but before the official declaration of the poll some days later. Of course, there might be incentives for a candidate to renounce their foreign allegiance prior to running for the office of President since this might be seen as politically fatal. Other disqualifications have been suggested, such as an age limit of 40. Would such a disqualification constitute a good reason for exclusion from the right to stand for office? Wisdom is a virtue but an age limit is arbitrary and discriminatory, an unnecessary restriction.

31 As happened in the 1980s with the election of Bobby Sands, who was currently serving a prison sentence for activities with the IRA. He died of a hunger strike for the political recognition of IRA prisoners. He did not receive state honours at his funeral.
32 Mayo, *An Introduction to Democracy*, p. 107.
33 Mayo, *An Introduction to Democracy*, p. 107.
34 C Saunders (2008) 'Implementing Models' (Paper presented at Planning for a Republic – The Legal Mechanic's Perspective, Perth, 29 November Session 2).
35 Mayo, *An Introduction to Democracy*, p. 139.
36 *Electoral Act 1918* (Cth) s 170(2) (b), (c) states a nomination is not valid unless the nominee deposits the sum required under subsection (3). *Electoral Act 1918* (Cth) s 170(3) (a) stipulates that the required sum for a nominee as a Senator is $1000. Section 170(3) (b) states the required sum for a nominee as a member of the House of Representatives is $500. Provision for refund for successful candidates and for forfeiture for unsuccessful candidates are found in *Electoral Act 1918* (Cth) s 173(1).
37 *Electoral Act 1918* (Cth) s 166(1) (b) requires the signatures of 50 people who are eligible to vote or the signature of the registered officer of a registered political party in order to make a valid nomination.
38 Winterton, 'The Resurrection of the Republic', p. 12.
39 Winterton, 'The Resurrection of the Republic', p. 12.
40 Mayo, *An Introduction to Democracy*, p. 139.
41 *Electoral Act 1918* (Cth) ss 166(1) (b), 126(2)(ca).
42 See Gallop Model mentioned by Winterton, 'The Resurrection of the Republic', pp. 11–12.
43 J Duffy 'Appendix 4: Overseas Studies: Ireland' in *An Australian Republic: The Options – the Appendices* (1993), p. 136.
44 Duffy, *An Australian Republic*, p. 136.
45 Duffy, *An Australian Republic*, p. 136.
46 Winterton, 'The Resurrection of the Republic', p. 12.
47 See Winterton, 'The Resurrection of the Republic', p. 12.
48 Mayo, *An Introduction to Democracy*, p. 62.
49 Mayo, *An Introduction to Democracy*, pp. 62–3.
50 PR Dudgeon & PM Hincks (2007) *Democracy Rules: an electoral*

education resource, Australian Electoral Commission, Commonwealth of Australia, p. 69.
51 Dudgeon & Hinks, *Democracy Rules: an electoral education*, p. 8; Saunders 'Implementing Models'.
52 Saunders, 'Implementing Models'.
53 Hunter, 'Working the Republic: Some Feminist Reflections', p. 61.
54 Hunter, 'Working the Republic: Some Feminist Reflections', p. 59.
55 Hunter, 'Working the Republic: Some Feminist Reflections', p. 61.
56 cf. Hunter, 'Working the Republic: Some Feminist Reflections', p. 59.
57 Hunter, 'Working the Republic: Some Feminist Reflections', p. 61.
58 Winterton, 'The Resurrection of the Republic', p. 14.
59 Winterton, 'The Resurrection of the Republic', p. 14.
60 Winterton, 'The Resurrection of the Republic', pp. 14–15.
61 Winterton, 'The Resurrection of the Republic', p. 15.
62 McKenna, *The Captive Republic*, p. 5.
63 Winterton, 'The Resurrection of the Republic', p. 5.
64 Mayo, *An Introduction to Democracy*, pp. 61–2.
65 N Bobbio (1987) *The Future of Democracy*, Polity Press, p. 8.
66 Mayo, *An Introduction to Democracy*, p. 5.
67 Sir O Dixon (1935) 'The Law and the Constitution', *Law Quarterly Review*, vol. 51, p. 597.
68 G Lindell (1986) 'Why is Australia's Constitution Binding? – The Reasons in 1900 and Now, and the Effect of Independence', *Federal Law Review*, vol. 16, p. 37.
69 See Lindell, 'Why is Australia's Constitution Binding', p. 37.
70 See Australian Constitution.
71 United States Constitution, preamble.
72 The Constitution of India, preamble.
73 See generally Krygier, 'Between Fear and Hope'.

Chapter 7

1 D Otto (2009) 'Pushing Feminism off the Map? International Law in Times of Crisis', Inaugural Professorial Lecture, (Lecture Presented at Melbourne Law School, 20 May).
2 G Agamben (2005) *State of Exception*, University of Chicago Press, p. 2. Agamben contends that the language of crises is 'not the exception', but rather is the norm, and that this 'state of exception' became established by the middle of the twentieth century, as the 'dominant paradigm of [modern] government'. Otto, 'Pushing Feminism off the Map?'
3 G Winterton (2001) *The Resurrection of the Republic*, Federation Press, p. 13.
4 B Jones (1999) 'Framing a New Australian Republic', Paper presented at Australian Academy of the Humanities, 30th Anniversary Symposium, 3 November 1999 in Australian Academy of the Humanities, *Proceedings 1999*, Southwood Press, p. 122.
5 J Howard (1994) 'Mr Keating's Mirage on the Hill: How the Republic, Like the Cheshire Cat, Came and Went' in *Upholding the Australian Constitution*, vol. 3: Proceedings of the Third Conference of The Samuel Griffith Society, pp. 115, 130–1.

6 M Krygier (1997) 'Between Fear and Hope', Boyer Lectures, 16 November.
7 Krygier, 'Between Fear and Hope'.
8 Krygier, 'Between Fear and Hope'.
9 C Schmitt (1985, 1922) 'Definition of Sovereignty' and 'The Problem of Sovereignty as the Problem of the Legal Form and of the Decision' in *Political Theology: Four Chapters of the Concept of Sovereignty*, MIT Press; Agamben, *State of Exception*.
10 *Criminal Code Act 1995* (Cth) division 104.
11 Otto, 'Pushing Feminism off the Map?'.
12 See G Patmore & J Whyte (1997) 'Imagining Constitutional Crises: Power and (Mis)behaviour in Republican Australia', *Federal Law Review*, vol. 25(1), pp. 181, 189.
13 See B Galligan (1991) 'The Vice-Regal Office in Australia' in *Sovereigns and Surrogates: Constitutional Heads of State in the Commonwealth*, (eds) D Butler & D Low, MacMillan, pp. 61, 85–97.
14 P Hanks, P Keyzer & J Clarke (2004) *Australian Constitutional Law: Materials and Commentary*, Butterworths, pp. 464–507.
15 See the discussion of the actions of Sir Joh Bjelke-Petersen in Galligan, 'The Vice-Regal Office in Australia', pp. 85–92.
16 See Patmore & Whyte, 'Imagining Constitutional Crises', p. 189.
17 To some, the term 'aggrandisement' may seem imprecise and unclear. However, I have provided examples to give content to this concept. Most importantly, the term serves another important function, which is to describe a kind of political experience and to enhance our political vocabulary. Also see B Galligan (1993) 'Regularising the Australian Republic', *Australian Journal of Political Science*, vol. 28, pp. 56, 57.
18 P Keating (1995) 'An Australian Republic: The Way Forward', (Speech delivered at Parliament House, Canberra, 7 June).
19 For a general discussion of the current legal and constitutional responsibilities of the head of state, see HV Evatt (1967) *The King and His Dominion Governors*, Cheshire; E Forsey 'The Present Position of the Reserve Powers of the Crown', in *Evatt and Forsey on the Reserve Powers*, Evatt (1990), Legal Books; Hanks et al, *Australian Constitutional Law*, pp. 498–507.
20 For theoretical discussion of legitimacy, see H Arendt (1963) *On Revolution*, Penguin; M Weber (1968) *Economy and Society: An Outline of Interpretive Sociology*, University of California Press; J Habermas (1975) *Legitimation Crisis*, Beacon Press.
21 Constitutional Convention: Transcript of Proceedings, Canberra, 12 February 1998, p. 846, (Malcolm Turnbull).
22 Keating, 'An Australian Republic'.
23 Keating, 'An Australian Republic'.
24 Office of the Prime Minister (1995) An Australian Republic: The Way Forward: Questions and Answers, 7 June, p. 9.
25 G Winterton (1993) 'The Evolution of a Separate Australian Crown', *Monash University Law Review*, vol. 19, pp. 1, 10.
26 See Winterton, *The Resurrection of the Republic*, p. 18; See, for example, the views cited ibid, at p. 37; C Saunders, 'Reflections on the Referendums', *ALSA Reporter* Summer 2000, pp. 5, 6.
27 See Winterton, *The Resurrection of the Republic*.

28 See Evatt, *The King and His Dominion Governors*, pp. 7–11, 286–92. See Winterton, 'The Evolution of a Separate Australian Crown', p. 46.
29 Keating, 'An Australian Republic'.
30 Forsey, 'The Present Position of the Reserve Powers', pp. lxxxiii–lxxxiv
31 Forsey, 'The Present Position of the Reserve Powers', pp. lxxxiii–lxxxiv.
32 But contrast AJ Ward (2000) 'Australia and Parliamentary Orthodoxy: A Foreign Perspective on Australian Constitutional Reform' (Paper presented in the Senate Occasional Lecture Series, Canberra, 18 June), p. 10. 'There is nothing so mysterious, so subtle, so nuanced about conventions that they cannot be written into law, once their purpose is clear.'
33 For High Court recognition of these principles, see, for example, *Australian Communist Party v Commonwealth* (1951) 83 CLR 1 at 193 per Dixon J; *Lange v Australian Broadcasting Corporation* (1997) 189 CLR 520. Various scholars have suggested ways of partially codifying the reserve powers. Saunders, 'Reflections on the Referendums', p. 6; Winterton, *The Resurrection of the Republic*, pp. 18–19; Patmore & Whyte, 'Imagining Constitutional Crises', pp. 197–203.
34 Three powers could be specified:
    1. The power to appoint a Prime Minister should be confined to the person most likely to be supported by a majority of members of the House of Representatives after a general election (Winterton, *The Resurrection of the Republic*, p. 18).
    2. The power of the head of state to refuse a dissolution requested by a Prime Minister should be limited to situations where:
        a. the House of Representatives has not met after a general election, unless it cannot elect the Speaker
        b. the Prime Minister 'has lost a constructive no-confidence motion'
        c. no-confidence motion has been proposed but not confirmed (Winterton, *The Resurrection of the Republic*, p. 19; Winterton 'The evolution of a Separate Australian Crown', p. 44).
    3. The power of the head of state to dismiss a Prime Minister or dissolve the Parliament and call a general election should operate only where a Prime Minister: insists on ignoring a vote of no-confidence; contravenes a fundamental constitutional provision or principle (notwithstanding a High Court decision confirming such infringement), or; does not heed requests to desist by the head of state ('if the matter has been held non-justiciable by the High Court'). Such breaches of the Constitution might include a refusal to summon Parliament or to call a general election when the parliamentary term has expired. Dismissal on the basis of a breach of a fundamental constitutional convention is a most contentious issue. The power might include dismissal based on deferral of supply by the Senate, as occurred in the 1975 constitutional crisis.
35 Office of the Prime Minister.
36 Former politicians who have recently departed politics have acted in aid of the public good; for example, the former Governor-General Bill Hayden.

37 Republican Advisory Council (1993) *An Australian Republic: The Options*, Australian Government Publishing Service, vol. 1, p. 56.
38 Winterton, *The Resurrection of the Republic*, p. 12. There is empirical evidence which indicates that voters themselves are not concerned that the candidate be a former politician. Winterton, *The Resurrection of the Republic*, p. 9.
39 Winterton, *The Resurrection of the Republic*, p. 19.
40 Winterton, *The Resurrection of the Republic*, pp. 19–20.
41 G Brennan (2008) 'The 16th Annual Lucinda Lecture: The Parameters of Constitutional Change' (Speech delivered at Monash University, 13 November).
42 The office has also been described as the 'ultimate constitutional umpire.'(J Howard [1999] 'Nothing to Gain, Everything to Lose', *The Australian*, 27 October, p. 8.) The following qualities have been attributed to the umpire function:

  Independence or security of tenure (Australian Electoral Commission [1999] *1999 Referendum Yes/No Case Pamphlet*, Commonwealth of Australia, p. 21.)

  Freedom from interference from anyone, acting in accordance with the powers in the Constitution and the conventions of the Crown (Howard, 'Nothing to Gain, Everything to Lose'.)

  Separation of the head of state from the Executive Government, preventing concentration of power in the executive, acting as a check and balance on executive power (see Legal and Constitutional References Committee, Senate, *The Road to a Republic*, August 2004, p. 121–4).
43 Winterton, *The Resurrection of the Republic*, p. 8.
44 The notion of enforcement is also troubling since enforcement requires ensuring observance of, or obedience to, fundamental principles. Ordinarily the enforcement of legal principles is the realm of the courts.
45 While the guarantor notion is a useful analogy to explain the function of the head of state in the current system of government, it is neither stated expressly in the Constitution nor is it an established unwritten convention. It is therefore arguable that the Governor-General has no such role at present. The republican debate and the proposals for a republican head of state provide a pertinent opportunity to define the role of a future President. For an earlier discussion of this conception see Patmore & Whyte, 'Imagining Constitutional Crises', pp. 198–200.
46 The Constitution is breached regularly, as evidenced by all the cases: see Hanks et al. Interestingly, the codes proposed by the Republican Advisory Committee (*An Australian Republic: The Options*), provide a procedure for the head of state to dismiss a Prime Minister for breaching a fundamental constitutional provision but do not define the meaning of the term 'fundamental'.
47 A precedent exists for the use of the term 'guarantor' in a constitution. In Article 5 of the French Constitution the term is used as a guarantee. The French President, amongst other things, is a 'guarantor of ... respect for Community agreements and for treaties'. While Article 5 provides a function that would go beyond the anticipated function of an Australian head of state, it illustrates

how the term 'guarantor' can operate in a constitutional context beyond the confines of contract law. The term 'guarantee' imposes a responsibility on the head of state for a designated function.
48 C Saunders 'Implementing Models' (2008) (Paper presented at Planning for a Republic – The Legal Mechanic's Perspective, Perth, 29 November, Session 2).
49 Saunders, 'Implementing Models'.
50 See Patmore & Whyte, 'Imagining Constitutional Crises'.

Chapter 8

1 *Referendum (Machinery Provisions) 1984* (Cth) s 11(1).
2 The '1999 survey' was a large-scale survey of 1000 people from each of NSW, Vic., Qld, WA, SA and Tas., 100 from ACT and 50 from NT. Sample was taken from Commonwealth Electoral Roll (after the roll closed on 8 October 1999 for the referendum). The results were weighted for representativeness and precision. Only weighted results are referred to in the body of the text. D J Gow, C Bean & I McAllister (2000) *Australian Constitutional Referendum Study, 1999: User's Guide for the Machine-Readable Data File*, Social Science Data Archives, pp. vii–x.
3 I would like to thank Clive Bean for his advice regarding this chapter. His comments on the framing of the survey questions, the popularity of the leaders, the dismissal procedure, and on why Australians were not interested in the Constitution were particularly helpful.
4 J Pike (2001) 'What the People Want, What They Really Really Want – To Elect a President Themselves', viewed 16 June 2009, <http://ozconstinfo.freehomepage. com/republic/survey.html>.
5 Interview with Greg Craven (Telephone interview, 9 February 2009).
6 Interview with Kim Beazley (Telephone interview, 11 December 2008).
7 Interview with John Howard (Telephone interview, 11 December 2008).
8 Gow et al, *Australian Constitutional Referendum Study*, p. 26.
9 Gow et al, *Australian Constitutional Referendum Study*, p. 25.
10 G Winterton (2001) *The Resurrection of the Republic*, Federation Press and Centre for International and Public Law, Law and Policy Paper No. 15.
11 Australian Electoral Commission (1999) *Yes/No Pamphlet*, p. 11, viewed 9 September 2005, <http://www.australianpolitics.com/issues/republic/>.
12 Australian Electoral Commission, *Yes/No Pamphlet*, p. 15.
13 Howard, 11 December 2008.
14 Interview with Phil Cleary (Telephone interview, 20 February 2009).
15 M Turnbull (1999) *Fighting for the Republic*, Hardie Grant Books, p. 119.
16 Interview with Kerry Jones (Telephone interview, 18 December 2008).
17 Interview with Sir David Smith (Telephone interview, 6 February 2009).
18 Gow et al, *Australian Constitutional Referendum Study*, p. 10.

19 Gow et al, *Australian Constitutional Referendum Study*, p. 33.
20 Australian Electoral Commission 1999, *Yes/No Pamphlet*, p. 9.
21 Turnbull, *Fighting for the Republic*, p. 103.
22 Only a few studies have been conducted. See Constitutional Commission (1988) *Final Report of the Constitutional Commission: Volume One*, Australian Government Publishing Service, p.43; See G Williams. 'Sifting the Ashes' in *Constitutional Politics: The Republic Referendum and the Future* (eds) J Warhurst & M Mackerras (2002), University of Queensland Press, pp. 131, 139.
23 Civics Expert Group (1994) *Whereas the People...: Civics and Citizenship Education – Report of the Civics Experts Group*, Australian Government Publishing Service, pp. 19, 143.
24 Jones, 18 December 2008.
25 Turnbull, *Fighting for the Republic*, p. ix.
26 Craven, 9 February 2009.
27 Craven, 9 February 2009.
28 Gow et al, *Australian Constitutional Referendum Study*, p. 26.
29 Gow et al, *Australian Constitutional Referendum Study*, p. 31.
30 I McAllister (2001) 'Elections Without Cues: The 1999 Australian Republic Referendum', *Australian Journal of Political Science*, vol. 36(2), pp. 247–69.
31 Australian Electoral Commission 1999: 9.
32 M Kirby (2000) 'The Australian Referendum on a Republic – Ten Lessons', *Australian Journal of Politics & History*, vol. 46, pp. 510, 528.
33 Australian Electoral Commission, *Yes/No Pamphlet*, p. 9.
34 Cleary, 20 February 2009.
35 Jones, 18 December 2008.
36 Gow et al, *Australian Constitutional Referendum Study*, pp. 18–19.
37 Australian Electoral Commission, *Yes/No Pamphlet*, p. 9.
38 Interview with Bob Charles (Telephone interview, 4 February 2009).
39 Beazley, 11 December 2008.
40 Cleary, 20 February 2009.
41 Gow et al, *Australian Constitutional Referendum Study*, p. 7.
42 Winterton, *The Resurrection of the Republic*, pp. 3–4.
43 McAllister, 'Elections Without Cues', p. 256.
44 Pike, 'What the People Want, What They Really Really Want'.
45 Australian Electoral Commission 1999, *Yes/No Pamphlet*, p. 21.
46 Gow et al, *Australian Constitutional Referendum Study*, p. 27.
47 Gow et al, *Australian Constitutional Referendum Study*, p. 26.
48 C Bean (2002) 'Political Personalities and Voting in the 1999 Australian Constitutional Referendum', *International Journal of Public Opinion Research*, vol. 14, pp. 459, 464.
49 Bean, 'Political Personalities and Voting', pp. 464–5.
50 H Irving (2000) 'The Republic Referendum of 6 November 1999', *Australian Journal of Political Science*, vol. 35, p. 112.
51 Bean, 'Political Personalities and Voting', p. 459.
52 Bean, 'Political Personalities and Voting', p. 460.
53 Bean *speculates* that combining the two popularity effects may have cost the Yes vote about 1.5 per cent of the total vote, 'not an inconsequential slice of the margin'. Malcolm Turnbull himself acknowledged that his personal popularity was affected by the No case. Bean, 'Political Personalities and Voting', p. 466. See

also S Bennett (2002–03) *The Politics of Constitutional Amendment*, Parliamentary Research Service, Commonwealth Parliament, Research Paper No. 11.
54 Irving, 'The Republic Referendum of 6 November 1999', pp. 111–12.
55 McAllister, 'Elections Without Cues', p. 247.
56 McAllister, 'Elections Without Cues', pp. 257–8.
57 B Tranter (2000) 'Referendum voting and support for an Australian Republic', Paper presented at The 2000 Conference of the Australasian Political Studies Association, Canberra, 3–6 October 2000, pp. 1–20, 5.
58 Tranter, 'Referendum voting and support', pp. 4–6.
59 'Although the size of the standardised estimates suggest that age was not a strong predictor of voting.'
60 Tranter notes that trust was the remaining characteristic after other characteristics.
61 Tranter, 'Referendum voting and support', pp. 5–6.
62 Irving 'The Republic Referendum of 6 November 1999', p. 113; Tranter, 'Referendum voting and support', p. 5.
63 Tranter, 'Referendum voting and support', p. 5.
64 Tranter, 'Referendum voting and support', p. 5.
65 Tranter, 'Referendum voting and support', p. 6.
66 See Turnbull, *Fighting for the Republic*, p. 210.
67 Gow et al, *Australian Constitutional Referendum Study*, p. 10.
68 Gow et al, *Australian Constitutional Referendum Study*, p. 25.

Chapter 9

1   JF Lyotard (1984) *The Postmodern Condition: A Report of Knowledge*, Manchester University Press.
2   R Appignanesi & C Garratt (2004) *Introducing Postmodernism*, Icon Books, p. 189.
3   Interview with Jason Yat Sen Li (Telephone interview 13 February 2009).
4   Interview with Kim Beazley (Telephone interview, 11 December 2008).
5   M Krygier 'Between Fear and Hope', Boyer Lectures, 16 November 1997, Lecture 2, viewed 11 March 2009, <http://www.abc.net.au/rn/boyerlectures/stories/1997/988491.htm>.
6   G Simpson (2009) 'Inaugural Professorial Lecture: War Crimes Trials, Solemnity and the Problem of Evil' (Lecture delivered at Melbourne Law School, 22 April).
7   Here are some examples of republican groups that I encountered at a recent seminar: Australian Republican Movement, Women for an Australian Republic, and The Real Republican Ltd (Direct Election Group) to name but a few.
8   D Otto (2009) 'Pushing Feminism off the Map? International Law in Times of Crisis', Inaugural Professorial Lecture (Lecture delivered at Melbourne Law School, 20 May).
9   See Otto, 'Pushing Feminism off the Map?'
10 Otto, 'Pushing Feminism off the Map?'
11 Otto, 'Pushing Feminism off the Map?'
12 DJ Gow, C Bean & I McAllister (2000), *Australian Constitutional*

Referendum Study, 1999: User's Guide for the Machine-Readable Data File, Social Science Data Archives, p. 26.
13 Commonwealth, Parliamentary Debates, Senate, 11 November 2008, 6541 (Bob Brown, Leader of the Australian Greens).
14 C Uhlmann (2008) 'Rudd talks regulation and republic', *AM*, ABC Radio, 21 April.
15 M Grattan (2008) 'The Turnbull Ascendancy – Liberal Leadership', *The Age*, 17 September.

Index

Aboriginal person, as head of state 122
Act of Settlement 1701 (UK) 107
Agamben, Georgio 145
agenda setting, for a republic 37–41, 200–4
American Revolution 34, 99
An Australian Republic: the Way Forward (Keating speech) 89–90, *see also* Keating model
ANZUS Treaty 18
appointment and removal procedures for head of state 46–7, 49, 93, 119–39, 142
  legitimacy of powers depending upon 153–6
  see also head of state; President
Asia-Pacific Economic Co-operation (APEC) 38
Australia Act 1986 (Cth) 19
Australian colonies, self-government push 13–14, 31–2
Australian Constitutional Convention Survey 1999 175–96
  implications for the future 194–6
Australian Labor Party (ALP) 17, 38, 190
Australian Republican Movement 25, 178
Australians for a Constitutional Monarchy 25, 178
Austria 125

Bagehot, Walter 63, 64, 69 n14
Beazley, Kim 52, 54–5, 56, 60, 185, 199
Bill of Rights 25
bipartisan parliamentary election of head of state 4
  legitimacy of role and 154–5
  parliamentary nominations 120–1
  see also head of state
Brown, Bob 204
Bryce, Quentin 123

Cabinet, decisions of and Governor-General's role 76–8

(233)

Canada 141
ceremonial role, of Governor-General 68–70
  see also Governor-General
Charles, Bob 53, 54, 56, 185
Charles, Prince 29
checks and balances 147–9
  see also political instability
citizenship 127
civic virtue 98
Civics Experts Report (1994) 181
Cleary, Phil 178, 184, 186
collusion, between head of state and others 162–3
colonial nationalism 16
common good and republicanism 11, 99–100
Commonwealth Games 183
Commonwealth, history and meaning of the term 9–10
Constitution
  alteration procedures 34–6
  conventions 95
  patriation of (bringing it home) 140–1
  rewriting 47–8
  safeguards for democracy 151
  sovereignising the people 140–1
  see also section 128
Constitution Act 1975 (Vic) 106
constitutional change for a republic 2, 31–62, 201–2
  choosing the question 51–7
  informing the people 57–61
  issues and agendas 37–41
  Keating model 46–8, 89–90
  misunderstanding and education 178–88, 195–6, 201
  1999 referendum model 48–9
  policy processes 41–5
  process 3, 33
  selecting the model 45–59
  Senate report model 49–50
  steps required 32
Constitutional Commission (1988) 67–8
Constitutional Convention (1998) 24–6, 39, 119–20, 156
Constitutional Council 165–7
Constitutional Crisis 1975 18, 79–87
constitutional design 3–4

constitutional guarantor of democratic continuity 168–9, 169–71, 201–2
constitutional guardian 167
constitutional monarchy 12, 96
constitutional umpire role 167–8
Corowa People's Conference 2001 28
counsel, advise and warn 75, 87
Craven, Greg 45, 176, 182–3
Cromwell, Oliver 9–10
Crown 106–9
crowned republic 105–6, 91, 109-110

Deakin, Alfred 16
Deane, William 69
defence and nationalism 17–18
democracy and referendum questions 196
Dibbs, George 16
direct democracy 6, 98, 115, 135–9
direct election and YES/NO vote 184–6, 195–7
direct election of head of state 50, 102, 115–16, 123–7, 135–9
  criticisms of 124, 137–8
  instability 146
  legitimacy of role and 156–7, 186, 202
  1999 referendum and 185
disloyalty and republicanism 12–13, 20, 103
dismissal
  of Whitlam government 18, 72, 79–87, 149
  political instability 147
  Prime Minister and President 184
Downer, Alexander 39
Durack, Peter 80

education 4, 60-1, 176, 181, 183, 188, 201
education levels and referendum support 191, 193–4, 201
  see also political education
elections, Governor-General's role 70–1
  see also bipartisan parliamentary elections; direct democracy; direct election of head

of state
English Constitution, The (Bagehot) 63–4
disqualifications, of people from head of state 132–4
executive appointment, of Governor-General 117–18
executive authority, of Governor-General 76
executive powers, of Governor-General 72–4

Federal Executive Council, advisory role 74
Federalism 35–6
Federation and republicanism 10
Fifield, Mitch 44
Fiji 149
Fisher, Andrew 58
fit and proper persons 127
folk politics 101
Fraser, Malcolm 80
Freeman, David 61, 58-61
French Revolution 13

Game, Philip 85
Garran, Robert 10, 74
generations and 1999 referendum support 191
Germany 132, 149
Governor-General
  acting on advice 74–6, 87, 166–7
  as Queen's representative 66–8
  ceremony and leadership 68–70
  constitutional crisis 79–86
  elections and inauguration 70–2
  executive authority 76–8
  executive powers 72–4
  legitimacy of 154
  reserve powers 78–9
  role of 65–79
  see also head of state
Greens 25, 204

Hasluck, Sir Paul 69
head of state
  Australian as 4, 90, 176–7, 195
  bipartisan parliamentary election model 4
  functions of 167–71
  Governor-General 66
  legitimacy of 154–6, 186, 201–2
  monarch's role 19, 66–8
  nomination 128–34
  popular sovereignty 139–41
  qualifications 127–8
  replacing the Queen, changing the political culture 91–6
  selecting 112–44
  voting system 135–9
  see also Governor-General; President
High Court 19
Hollingsworth, Peter 65
Howard, John 23, 24–8
  Constitutional Convention 42–3
  direct election 146
  keeping republic on the agenda 39
  question for 1999 referendum 51, 54, 55–6
  referendum campaign 59
Hudson, Wayne 104
Humphries, Barry 125

Iceland 130
idealism and republicanism 99–102, 199–200
India 141
Indigenous peoples 25
information, on referendum issue 57–61
  see also education
interest based politics 149–50
Ireland 125, 132
Irish independence movement 13–14

Jones, Barry 146
Jones, Kerry 25, 178, 182, 184

Keating model 46–8, 89–90, 156–7
Keating, Paul 4, 21, 22, 23–4, 37–8, 42, 89–90, 105, 110–11, 165
Kerr, Sir John 18, 79–86, 92–3
knowledge of Constitution and NO vote 180–5, 196–7
  see also education
Krygier, Martin 112

labour movement, inequality and republicanism 14–15
Lang, Jack 85, 149
leadership role, of Governor-

General 68–70
legitimacy of President 93–4, 139–41, 150–1, 152–6
Liberal Party and republic 24, 39, 40, 190
Lincoln, Abraham 27
loyalty and nationalism 12–13, 16–17, 103

McAllister, Ian 184, 190
McClelland Robert 55, 56
McGarvie, Richard 28
McKenna, Mark 103, 104
Madison, James 99, 120
maintenance of system 177–8
mandate, of head of state versus Parliament 135
  see also legitimacy
Mayo H.D. 127- 9
Menzies, Sir Robert 18
minimalist approach 89–111, 202
monarchy as head of state 19
  see also Crown; head of state; Queen
Moore, Harrison 36
Murphy, Justice Lionel 96

National Australasian Conventions 16
nationalism 4, 16–17, 38
neutrality and participation
  selecting head of state 113–14, 137–8, 141–4
9/11 145
1999 referendum model 49–50
nomination, of head of state 128–34
  by Parliament 131–4
  restricted 129–31
  see also head of state; President
Paine, Thomas 13
Parkes, Sir Henry 15
Parliament
  dissolution of 78
  powers of and referendum 36
parliamentary appointment of head of state 119–123, 142
parliamentary democracy 114
Parliamentary Joint Select Committee
  Bill for referendum question 51, 52–3

Parliamentary representatives
  amending Constitution 35
  role in republican discussion 202–3
parliamentary republics 125–6
participation 112
  selecting head of state and 113–14, 141–4
patriation 140, 143
patronage and symbolism 123
Pike, John 187
plebiscite program 28, 40, 43–4, 204
policy process, for constitutional change 41–5
political education, lack of 181, 196–7, 201
  see also education
political culture, changing by shift to a republic 91–6
political freedoms 97–8
political instability, 145–73, 201–3
political leaders, perceptions of and 1999 referendum question 189–90
politicians, distrust of 184, 189–90, 195–6
popular choice 6–7
popular sovereignty 139–41
Portugal 125, 130
power of head of state
  abuse of 146
  checks and balances 149–50, 156–71
  election models and popular sovereignty 134–41, 143
  rival source of 146
  see also legitimacy
preferential voting 135
President
  adopting the term 92
  advice of Constitutional council 165–6
  appointment and removal procedures 46–7, 49, 93, 119–39, 142
  authority of 121–2
  broadening authority 122, 134–9
  candidates 126
  codifying restraints on 162
  constraining abuse of power by

160–6
constitutional constraints 156–67
direct election 50, 123–6, 134–9
eligibility for 46
functions 167–71
Keating model for removal of 156–7
legitimacy of powers of 93–4, 139–41, 143, 146, 150, 152–6, 159, 186, 202
nomination 48, 128–34
parliamentary nomination 119–22, 136–142
popular sovereignty 139–41
powers 47
qualifications 127–8
restricting time in office 164–5
rewriting Constitution 47–8
States rights and a republic 47
voting for 135–9
see also Governor-General; head of state

public education, 1999 referendum 57–61, 178–88, 197

public opinion
Australian as head of state 176–7
maintaining current system 177–80
Prince Charles 29
referendum question 55, 57–61, 174–97

Queen
as head of state 66–8, 106–9
of Australia 68
replacing as head of state 91–6, 106–9
symbolic role 1, 12, 18–19

Quick, Sir John 10, 74

rebellion and republicanism 12, 20
referendum, responsible government 36
see also republican referendum (1999)
referendum (1967) 100
Reid, George 87
religion and referendum support 191

representative democracy, definition 5–6
see also parliamentary representatives

republic
Corowa People's Conference 2001 28
crowned 105–9
what type 22
republican referendum (1999) 1–2
bipartisan model 4
campaign around 59–61
defeat of and questions raised 27, 39
leaders opinions 177–96
misunderstanding of changes proposed 183
other political and social factors influencing 188–94
public opinions at the time 176–96
removal of President 156
the question 26–7, 51–7
republicanism 97–8
avoidance of the term 12–19
defined 8
destabilising effects? 145–73
Federation 11–12
history in Australia 3, 103–4
philosophy of 97-102
self-belief in importance of 199–200

Republic Advisory Committee (1993) 23, 42, 43, 105

reserve powers of head of state 78–9, 169
see also power of head of state

responsible government 35
and appointed head of state 117–18
see also parliamentary democracy

revolution and republicanism 12, 20
Rights of Man (Paine) 13
Road to a Republic (Senate report) 28, 40, 43–4
Roxon, Nicola 44
Royal prefix, symbolism of 108–9
Rudd, Kevin 28–9, 40, 41, 44, 203, 204–5

Saunders, Cheryl 58, 141
section 128 26, 34–6, 61–2
   see also Constitution;
      constitutional change
sedition 12–13
self-interest and politicians 99–102
   see also politicians, distrust of
Senate 28, 35–6, 43–4, 204
   authority 79
Senate report model 49–50
Smith, Sir David 72, 81–2, 179
social fabric, Crown's symbolic role 108–9
Statute of Westminster Adoption Act 1942 (Cth) 17
Stone, Adrienne 95
suffrage 15, 127–8
Sunstein, Cass 98
supply bills, blocking of 79, 85
symbolism
   and the Crown 108–9
   of the President 122

terrorism 144, 147
Tranter, B. 192, 193
Turnbull, Malcolm 26, 38, 40, 178, 182, 202, 204–5
   Constitutional Convention 43
   2020 Summit 28–9, 41, 44

Turnbull, Reginald 80

United States of America 141
   and Australia 18
universal suffrage 127–8

values, importance of 112–14, 143
Victoria, Queen of England 10, 14, 17
virtue 98, 101
voter understanding, of constitutional change 4
   see also education; political education
voting rights, for head of state 135–9

Watson, Don 21, 23
Whitlam, Gough 18, 72, 79–87
Williams, George 50
Winterton, George 124, 146
World War II and British Empire 17–18

Yat-Sen Li, Jason 199
Yes and No case, information on 57–61, 178–88
   see also political education